Teaching Children about Sex

Teaching Children about Sex

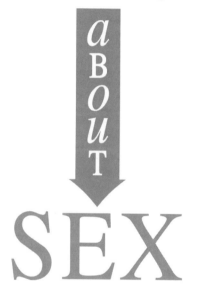

using the Temple as your Guide

Cherri Brooks

CFI
An imprint of Cedar Fort, Inc.
Springville, Utah

ISBN 13: 978-1-4621-1549-5

Published by CFI, an imprint of Cedar Fort, Inc.
2373 W. 700 S., Springville, UT 84663
Distributed by Cedar Fort, Inc., www.cedarfort.com

LIBRARY OF CONGRESS CATALOGING-IN-PUBLICATION DATA

Brooks, Cherri, 1981- author.
Teaching children about sex / Cherri Brooks.
pages cm
Includes bibliographical references and index.
ISBN 978-1-4621-1549-5 (alk. paper)
1. Sex instruction for children--Religious aspects--Church of Jesus Christ of Latter-day Saints. 2. Sex--Religious aspects--Church of Jesus Christ of Latter-day Saints. I. Title.

BX8643.S49B76 2015
241'.664071--dc23

2014043944

Cover design by Shawnda T. Craig
Cover design © 2015 Lyle Mortimer
Edited and typeset by McKell Parsons and Jessica B. Ellingson

Printed in the United States of America

10 9 8 7 6 5 4 3 2 1

Printed on acid-free paper

For Trevor, my someone

Contents

Introduction

I taught a parenting course at South Dakota State University. While I was doing research for various sections of the course, I decided it would be essential to discuss teaching children about sex. This was not covered in the course textbook, along with other topics I thought were important, like teaching children about financial responsibility. I found wonderful resources in various places for teaching children about financial responsibility in age-appropriate ways. I thought I would have the same experience when I researched teaching children about sex. However, I could find little information regarding age-appropriate discussions on sex. I had limited time and was disappointed in the information I was able to present to the class. Although this information was positive, it was vague. It didn't give me any idea what and when to teach *my* children about sex. As a result, I began thoroughly researching age-appropriate ways to teach children about sexuality in an effort to prepare my children for living in a sexualized world.

The research I gathered was positive but also seemed to lack a vital component. As a member of The Church of Jesus Christ of Latter-day Saints, I wanted information I should teach my children that would also convey the spiritual and sacred nature of sexuality. Most of what I found ignored any spiritual component of sexuality.

In fact, many resources seemed to convey the idea that parents should just accept that since so many teens are having sex, their teens are going to do it whether parents like it or not. The message seemed to suggest that parents should expect that their teen will be having sex. However, we *can* teach our children about sexuality and do it with the expectation that they will understand the sacred nature of sex and have the self-control to wait until marriage.

Sexuality is a difficult subject to discuss with children. I believe many parents avoid the subject unless there is a compelling reason to talk about it. As I talk with adult friends about how they learned about sex, I have found their experiences similar to my own. My parents did not discuss sexuality with me. Most often, it seemed, discussions about sexuality occurred around dating or engagement, *after* most children and youth have incorrect or worldly ideas about sexuality. However, parents are the greatest source of sexual knowledge for their child. Parents are a child's most effective teacher. They have the benefit of intimately knowing a child's personality and have the greatest opportunity for spontaneous teaching moments. They are the example children follow. Children may not always look like they are watching, but they are observing the minute details of our lives. Children also look to parents for information. Have you, as a parent, ever had your child ask you, "Why?" The great thing is that they believe you when they are young!

Since parents are children's greatest source for sexual knowledge, they need a resource for appropriate information. This book is designed as a guide for appropriately responding to and answering children's questions about sex. The assumption is that parents have a good relationship with their child and are exercising effective parenting. Effective parenting includes high-quality communication (including listening), expectations for behavior (rules), monitoring, consequences for inappropriate behavior, and an overall attitude of love and respect in the home (see *A Parent's Guide*). Without these essential parenting practices, conveying the spiritual aspects and sacred nature of sexuality may be diminished.

The focus of this book is teaching appropriate sexual behavior with the correct attitude. Sexual behavior and sexuality are interconnected. However, there is a distinction between sexual behavior and sexuality. Sexual behavior is personal conduct, and sexuality is an attitude (see *Sex and Sexuality*). Sexuality includes not only sexual behavior but also a person's attitudes and feelings about gender, sexual orientation, and body image. Sexuality is influenced by culture, gender, religion, and a host of other agents. Because it is difficult to discuss all the factors that shape sexuality, this book is intended to concentrate on the Latter-day Saint religious views that shape sexuality, which will include attitudes and behavior.

I decided that I would like to share the information I have researched with an added spiritual component. My views are not licensed by The Church of Jesus Christ of Latter-day Saints but are guided by their principles. Members of this Church are taught by spiritual leaders that "parents are responsible to teach their children about procreation (the process of conceiving and bearing children)" (*Gospel Principles*, 225). In fact, if we are not teaching our children about virtue and morality, leaders have indicated that we "shirk" in our duties as parents to "avoid the stress" of teaching this vital conduct (*A Parent's Guide*, 33).

The Church has some guidelines and information about teaching children about sexuality in chapter 39 of the *Gospel Principles* manual. *A Parent's Guide* is also an excellent Church-approved resource for teaching children about sexuality. I strongly recommend reading through *A Parent's Guide*, possibly before or during your reading of this book. There are also various talks by prophets, apostles, and other leaders on different sexuality topics, such as homosexuality and kissing. We need inspiration when we talk about such a beautiful and tender subject with our children. This book is designed to guide parents in following their spiritual leaders and to promote teaching children about sex.

Latter-day Saints are taught that they cannot receive inspiration until *after* they have studied the information available (D&C 9:8). This book is an effort to help you study the topic of sexuality so that when your child has questions or you feel like you need to address this topic, you will have the knowledge you need to receive the inspiration to answer your child's questions appropriately.

I'll begin with exploring an understanding of the body as a temple. The next section includes general advice for discussing sexuality with children of all ages. Then I'll address what is appropriate to teach children in various age groups. These age groups consist of curious learners (ages 0–5 years), concrete learners (ages 6–8 and 9–11), and conduct learners (12+ and premarital). These sections will provide information about what is appropriate or expected behavior at that age, typical questions for that age group and possible answers, and ideas for discussions about sexuality. I will also address the special topics of homosexuality and sexual abuse, harassment, and rape. The last chapter will be devoted to additional resources for parents in teaching their child about sexuality. It is my hope that this guide will be useful for you as you help your child understand and shape their sexual behaviors and attitudes.

SECTION 1

BUILDING A SEXUAL EDUCATION FOUNDATION

1

Temple Perspective

"My body is a temple, and you don't have a recommend!"

—Author Unknown

"What? know ye not that your body is the temple of the Holy Ghost which is in you, which ye have of God, and ye are not your own?" (1 Corinthians 6:19). Many teenagers and parents use a phrase similar to "My body is a temple, and you don't have a recommend" to combat pressure to engage in inappropriate sexual activity before marriage. Sometimes this is said with seriousness, sometimes in jest. However, do our teens really *know* what it means that their body is a temple of God? Do they know enough about their body to know how to use it correctly? Is this the only information you have given them about sex, to be abstinent?

You may think, *Yes, my teens know that their body is a temple and they shouldn't have sex before marriage.* I believe that often we assume our kids know exactly what we expect them to know and do. However, have you ever had a misunderstanding with your child? Have you ever expected something of them that they didn't complete, and then later found out that they had no idea you expected this of them? Maybe we expect them to clean out the sink when they are finished with the dishes. How does your child know that? Is there an inherent drive to clean out the sink when the dishes are done? I would say probably not. How do they know this is your expectation? You tell them.

My daughter and I were enrolled in a "Mommy and Me" gymnastics class when she was young. The instructor would tell us the steps and expected us to guide our children through them. The children were right with us when she explained her expectation. One day I started helping my daughter on the balance beam as the first step in the sequence. Next, she was to perform a V-sit. After the balance beam, she started to wander off to get a ball. The other parents were having similar results. The teacher reminded us that the children needed the next step explained to them while they finished the first step. This helped them prepare for the next step and know the expectation, making them less likely to wander off. I should have known this! I chastised myself for forgetting how young children learn. I knew my daughter needed me to tell her the expectation, but I had forgotten and assumed she knew what needed to be done next because there were visual reminders on the floor guiding the children to the next step. She had also been present during the instructor's explanation. However, she was not cognitively aware of all that was expected of her. She needed to be told as we moved through the steps.

Children also need to be *told* about sexuality. They do not always remember or understand the expectations you demand of them, even if they know the end product (abstinence until marriage). Some children do not even know the definition of sex, let alone understand the definition of abstinence. Assuming our children *know* is dangerous. Assumptions often lead to misunderstandings because they are based on what we *think* our kids know, not what they *do* know.

Contemplate for a moment. When do we teach children the definition of sex? What do we say? What kind of kissing is appropriate before marriage? When is it okay to hold hands? How far is too far? What does love mean, and what does it feel like? What should teenagers do when they have feelings of love? How can they say no to sex without having their boyfriend, girlfriend, or friends think they are not cool? Teens may know not to have sex before marriage, but they may not understand other factors associated with the body and relationships that are crucial for making wise choices. It is your job to teach them the facts and your expectations for their behavior based on those facts.

Consider sexual knowledge and behavior in the context of temple preparation. Before an individual is permitted to go into the temple, there are some preparatory steps taken to get that individual ready for entrance into the Lord's house. Children are taught from the time they are small that the temple is a beautiful place they will attend in the future. They are taught to appreciate the beauty and feelings associated with the temple from the outside. As children grow older, they are taught that there are special things that happen in the temple and that they need to prepare for the temple by behaving in a certain way. Teenagers are able to participate in certain ordinances in the temple when they reach an age appropriate to understand and participate in certain activities (12 years old). They also need to follow certain guidelines to enter the temple. As youth mature, they continue to be taught that they need to behave in a certain way to keep going to the temple. They are encouraged to look forward to other ordinances they can perform as a young adult. Just before a young adult is permitted to go to other areas of the temple, they go through a more formal temple preparation course. The course teaches them certain information that will enable them to be more fully prepared for temple ordinances. Then they are finally able to take part in the full blessings of the temple. This is a brief overview of how an individual is prepared for the temple.

Viewing the body as a temple, let's use the temple preparation above as a comparison for teaching our children about their bodies and sex. Small children are taught that their body is beautiful and can do many things. They are taught to do good with their bodies by helping others and exercising their mind and body. As children grow, they are taught that there are special ways to use their bodies, but they will wait to use their bodies in those ways until the appropriate time later in life. They are taught to prepare for these special moments by behaving in a certain way. Teenagers continue to be taught to control their appetites and prepare for the other uses of their bodies as they reach an appropriate stage in life. They are also able to participate in certain activities when they reach an appropriate age (16 years old). These activities will most likely consist of dating, hugging, and holding hands. They look forward to the time they can use their bodies in other ways to show love with one special person. Before they are permitted to use their bodies in this way, a formal ceremony of marriage is necessary. Then they are finally able to take part in the full blessings of sexual expression. I have broken down the comparison with some added details in a table to illustrate the similarities side-by-side.

TEMPLE	BODILY TEMPLE
Children learn to appreciate the beauty and sacred feelings associated with the temple.	Children learn to appreciate the beauty of their body and the various feelings their bodies can experience.
Children learn that they will attend the temple someday when they are older.	Children learn they can do many things with their body, some of which they can do when they get older (jump rope, ride a bike, sexual intercourse).
Children learn to keep the temple beautiful by being respectful of the outside (keeping up grounds, no graffiti).	Children learn to keep their bodies beautiful by treating it in a certain way (exercise, eat right, no tattoos).
Children learn to speak about the temple in a reverent way.	Children learn to speak about the body in a reverent way (refrain from potty humor or teasing about bodies).
Children learn that all temples are beautiful and unique and should be treated with the same respect.	Children learn that all people (bodies) are beautiful and unique and they should treat all bodies with the same respect.

Temple	Bodily Temple
Children are taught that there are certain ordinances that happen in the temple (baptisms, endowment, sealings), but they need to wait until a particular age or event (mission, marriage) to participate.	Children are taught that there are certain ways they can use their bodies (holding hands, kissing, sexual expression), but they need to wait until a particular age or event (dating, marriage) to use their bodies in these ways.
Entrance is permitted to certain areas of the temple at age 12.	Dating, hugging, holding hands, and certain activities are permitted for youth at age 16.
Youth are given the behavioral expectation that they will remain worthy of the temple by following certain guidelines (clean language, modesty in dress).	Youth are given the behavioral expectation that they will treat themselves and those whom they date in a certain way and follow guidelines (being respectful, adhering to curfews).
Youth are given the spiritual expectation that they will understand the purpose of and proper time for temple attendance and be developing their spirituality (reading scriptures, praying) in preparation for entrance.	Youth are given the spiritual expectation that they will understand the purpose of and proper time for sexual expression and be developing relationships (dating, friendships) in preparation for marriage.
Young adults or adults set a date for entrance and begin preparations.	Young adults or adults set a date for marriage and begin preparations.
The temple preparation course is taken before entrance to holier parts of the temple is permitted.	A ceremony of marriage is required before sexual intercourse is permitted.
Adults continue to attend the temple to strengthen the family and personal spirituality.	Adults continue sexual intercourse to strengthen the marital relationship and have children.

One of the purposes of the temple is to "play a role in the hallowed, redemptive work of salvation" (see Uchtdorf, "Temple Blessings"). In the temple, we are acting in a role that will aid in an individual's salvation. Likewise, as we participate in sexual relationships with our spouse, we are playing a role in the "redemptive work of salvation." We are using our bodies in a way that can create a body for a spirit child of Heavenly Father. This child needs a body to fulfill his or her purpose on earth and work toward his or her own salvation. Without a body, this child's path to salvation is frustrated. Thus you and your spouse are participating in a part of this child's redemption.

This illustration demonstrates that teaching children about sexuality is similar to teaching them about the temple. Instruction starts simple and begins at a young age. As children grow older, they are taught more and allowed to do more, but the ultimate prize is rewarded after a lot of preparation. In addition, we are often counseled to "stand in holy places" (D&C 45:32). The temple is a holy place, and our body is a holy place. Anytime we are speaking with our children about their bodies, we are standing on holy ground. The feelings, words, tone, and spirit should reflect the ground upon which we stand. If you dismiss a sexual question, you are dismissing the opportunity to teach them about holy ground. Would you reject a question they asked about the temple? I believe you would not. You should also not dismiss a question about their bodies, which are also holy temples.

Who is teaching and preparing your children for using *their* temples correctly? We want to believe it's us, but kids are learning and hearing about sex very early. My friend's child came home one day after first grade and asked her, "What's sex?" If you are not talking to your child about sex, who is? What are they learning? If you tell them you'll discuss it when they're older, who will teach them in the meantime, and what will they learn? They are most likely not learning about the sacred nature of sexual behavior, nor standing on holy ground as they hear about it. You can place their feet on holy ground as you take the initiative to teach them the proper respect for and expectations regarding sexuality.

2

Building a Foundation

"Attitudes are contagious. Are yours worth catching?"

—Dennis and Wendy Mannering

Before you begin to discuss sexuality with your child, there are a few things to consider. You need to build a foundation (sexuality basics) before your structure can take shape (children's sexual knowledge, attitudes, and behavior). If your foundation is strong, the structure can withstand the blows created by a sexualized world. If you build a durable foundation for talking about sexuality, your child will be better equipped to understand sexuality and control sexual behavior. We begin with your attitude and comfort level.

Admitting Your Attitude

When I was young, my dad occasionally took me on daddy-daughter dates. I remember one date in particular: we went to a café called The Chatterbox. This was my opportunity to talk with my dad one-on-one without vying for his attention with my other five siblings. I remember absolutely nothing from the conversation, though I can still recall that I felt loved. He could have spent the whole time telling me he loved me, but what I remember is *feeling* loved. Many times children *see* and *feel* more than *hear* what we are telling them.

A self-evaluation of your own attitudes about sexuality can provide areas in which you might need to fine-tune some of your feelings. Children may pick up messages you don't realize you're sending. For example, when a child is told, "Don't touch that!" (referring to a genital part and said in a shocked, disgusted, or angry tone), what message is the child getting? The child may not even remember what they are being told, but they may remember their genitals as a place associated with shock, disgust, or anger. Now, imagine that attitude carrying on to a marital relationship. There's no wonder why it's uncomfortable to talk about sex when the feelings associated with those body parts are shock, disgust, anger, or any other negative emotion. The physical pleasure is still tainted by the negative feelings. Your intent may be to keep parts of their body sacred by teaching them not to touch their sacred genitals when it's inappropriate. However, tone of voice, facial expression, and body language may not be conveying exactly what you intend your child to learn.

There are subtle ways you convey attitudes about sexuality and may not realize it. My friend was driving in the car with her three-year-old daughter. Her daughter was into spelling, although most of her "spellings" were not really words. One day she asked, "Mom, what does P-O-R-N spell?"

Mumbled responses, gasps of surprise, and comments in a disapproving tone all convey a message and show your attitude. Each of those responses essentially tells the child that this is a bad word that should not be discussed. It is also telling the child you are uncomfortable with this word. A child at this age has no concept of pornography and will not understand your response. You can say, "That spells porn because *p* says 'puh.' Let's try another one." This is very matter-of-fact. The child is not asking about sexuality, just sounds. You could also respond, "That spells a word I'm uncomfortable saying because it's not a nice word. Let's try another one."

A self-evaluation can also help you understand your own ideas about sexuality and how you would like to convey a sacred attitude about sexuality to your children. A self-evaluation will help you realize what you want your attitude to be and make you aware of how you are portraying that attitude to your children. You need not share the answers to your questions with your children. It might be helpful to discuss some of them with a spouse or the child's other parent. However, this is just a self-evaluation. Ask yourself the following questions:

- How did my parents respond when I touched my genitals as a child?
- How long did I bathe with an opposite-sex sibling? How did I feel about it? How do I feel about my opposite-sex children bathing together?
- How did I first learn about sex? Who told me about sex? What did I feel when I first learned about sex?
- What is sex for? What role does it play in my life?
- How do I feel about my own sex life?
- What do I think is key for a good, healthy sex life? Is there anything I would like to change about my sex life?
- What attitude would I like my child to have toward sex?
- How do I respond when my child is touching their genitals? How do I feel about it?
- How do I respond when I see something sexual that is inappropriate? Why do I respond in the way I do? How do I feel during these experiences?
- How do I respond when my child sees something sexual that is inappropriate? Why do I respond the way I do? How do I think my child felt? How would I feel if my parent responded to me the way I responded to my child? What do I think my child learned from my response?

This is not a comprehensive list of questions, but it's a start toward understanding how you feel about sex. I suggest that you refer to *A Parent's Guide* for a wonderful example showing a parental response to a sexuality issue. Take special note of the attitude of the parent. A young boy is introduced to pornography through a friend (12–13). The response by the parent indicates a certain attitude toward not only sexuality but also his child. He first asks the child questions about how it felt to look at the pictures. Then the parent tries to see things from his son's perspective (it would have been difficult to tell a friend he didn't want to look). Then he tells his son how he feels about pornography. They discuss ways the child could handle such situations in the future. How would you respond if your child were introduced to pornography? What does this convey about your attitude toward sexuality and the sacredness of the body?

Next, be aware of how you respond when another person or your child is in a situation where sexuality is involved. Do you cringe when the lady in the next stall in a public bathroom reminds her daughter to wipe her vulva after urinating? Do you try to avert your gaze and hide your child's view when two teenagers are kissing at the mall? What kind of attitude is this conveying? Your child may see more than you think and take your silence, cringing, or disgust as a lesson in sexuality. This is most likely not the message you want to convey. For example, when two teenagers are kissing at the mall, you could say, "That kind of kissing is important for two people when they're married or in a committed relationship. It's not appropriate here in a crowded mall for two people so young." What message are you giving them now? What is your attitude conveying? What are they learning about sexuality?

Distress and Discomfort

There are reasons why talking about sexuality can be uncomfortable. Sexuality is sacred. It is private. It is meant to be intimate. We don't talk about certain things regarding the temple outside the temple walls because they are sacred. We don't want to defile what is sacred. Sex is also sacred to a relationship, and we don't want to defile it or our spouse by discussing it outside of the marital relationship, especially with our children.

Sexuality can also be uncomfortable to discuss for a number of other reasons. For most people, it's just awkward and unnerving. Children should be innocent and not have to worry about the responsibility that comes with sex, and it's hard to discuss it with them. They do not fully understand it. It can also be uncomfortable for kids. However, many kids don't start to feel uncomfortable with it until they are approaching puberty. This is great news because that means there's a window of opportunity for our child not to contribute to the awkwardness of a conversation about sex. It will mostly be our feelings creating a barrier in the conversation. Just because a conversation is awkward doesn't mean we shouldn't have it. It just takes more courage.

If you or your children are uncomfortable discussing sexuality, it is okay to admit you're uncomfortable. You can say, "This is something hard for me to talk about because it is so special and sacred, but it is important. I want to talk with you about this, even if it is uncomfortable." You could also tell your children that because it's a little embarrassing or awkward, you may hesitate a little bit. Tell them this doesn't mean you don't want to talk about sex, you just need more time to find the right words. It's appropriate to ask them to be patient with you as you describe something or answer a question about sexuality. If your children seem uncomfortable, you can ask them if they are uncomfortable and why they might feel that way.

Discussing sexuality with children doesn't have to be awkward, embarrassing, or uncomfortable. It can be a loving, enriching experience. If you teach your child about sexuality from birth, in the right time and right way, it can feel more natural and pleasant. There may still be awkward and embarrassing moments, but the overall feelings can be comfortable. This invites your child to come back and ask questions.

I have a good friend whose father sat him and one of his brothers down to have a sex talk. He was about 12 years old and his brother was about 9 years old. He said he was terribly uncomfortable with the conversation but very interested in what his father was saying. He said his brother was open and full of questions and didn't seem uncomfortable. My friend had entered puberty while his brother was still at an age where the embarrassment associated with sexuality was not as pronounced. My friend was uncomfortable, but he *did* want to hear what his father had to say. In fact, he said he was fascinated and curious about his father's explanation of sex. Children want to hear about their bodies and all they can do, even if it's uncomfortable. And there are ages where the comfort level is greater, usually before puberty.

When you take the time to evaluate your attitude, you can discover areas where you might need to make adjustments. This can lead to enriching experiences as you discuss sexuality with your child. Even if there are awkward moments, you can build a solid foundation with a sacred attitude toward sex.

3

The Beginning

"First we make our habits, then our habits make us."

—Charles C. Noble

Understanding your attitudes and feeling comfortable discussing sexuality are just part of the foundation you are building. Begin as soon as your child is born and teach specific information while discussing standards and teaching responsibility in relationships. Doing these things effectively shape your child's sexual attitudes, knowledge, and behavior.

Educate Early

How old is your child the first time you take them to church? How many times do you take them to church? Do they get all the information they need from a one-time exposure? You know that's not the way it works. You take them to church as soon as you feel comfortable your newborn will be safe enough from various germs found in public. Then you take them regularly, unless sickness, travel, or other occasional issues prevent church attendance. Why do you do this? You do it because you know they can't understand everything all at once. They need multiple exposures to get all the information they need to understand more complex information. You also do it because you know this will shape good habits.

Why is it that we feel we need to give children "the big talk" once they are around the age of 10? Do you remember exactly what you learned in your primary class when you were ten years old? The answer is probably no. Children need to hear things more than once, just like adults. This teaching starts when they are young. When you start talking with your children about sexuality from the time they are young, you are the person having the most say in what you teach your children. What they start learning at school or other times when you are not around they will fit into the foundation you have set for them or discard information that will not fit into that foundation.

Now, you don't need to explain the mechanics of sex to your three-year-old child. Remember, this is like learning about the temple. You don't explain what the endowment is until a basic foundation is set. This has probably started long before learning about the endowment. It starts simply, letting children enjoy the beauty of the temple from the outside and teaching them that they will go inside one day. Basically, for young children to start learning about sexuality, you name body parts correctly, show them love in appropriate ways, and encourage their gender role development (see *A Parent's Guide*; *Gospel Principles*). These are the important basics for young children. As they grow older, more detail is given for various aspects of sexuality, just as they learn more details about the temple as they mature.

Specifics and Standards

Bodily functions and processes are interesting for children. Ears are for hearing. Eyes are for seeing. Hands and skin are for feeling. Tongues are for tasting. Penises and vulvas are for urination. Breasts are for feeding a baby. Vaginas are for birth. Children are interested in why we have parts of our bodies. Explaining why we have each body part can help children feel more respect for all parts of their bodies.

Children need facts or specifics that are presented simply. Facts should include anatomically correct information as well as the mechanics and expectations associated with sexual behavior. My brother-in-law knew one little boy who was taught his penis was called a "pickle." One day the little boy was at a friend's house for lunch, and the mother asked if the boy wanted her to cut his pickle. The poor child was scared she wanted to cut his penis off! I have another friend whose child called genitals "delicates." This friend was trying to teach her child that the genitals are special, as suggested in her choice of label for the genitals. Many parents I've talked with describe the anatomically correct names of body parts as "feeling dirty" when they say the proper name. Satan has done a terrific job making these sacred body parts sound "dirty." But who named our body parts? Heavenly Father has named these parts, and when we say the proper names, we should be reminded that He has given us these parts with these names for an amazing purpose.

Our spiritual leaders have taught us that we need to talk with our children "frankly but reverently" and use anatomically correct names for body parts and how the body works (*Gospel Principles*, 225). This will help children mature with less shame for their bodies and their bodies' functions. In addition, jargon for body parts and functions disrespects this temple that houses our spirit and is made in the image of God (see *A Parent's Guide*).

Facts are not the only things children need to be taught; they also need to be taught values regarding sexuality. This is one problem with leaving the school system to teach children about bodies, maturation, and sexuality. The school system generally focuses on the facts and ignores education on values or standards. Consider this quote for educators from the Planned Parenthood website: school-based sex education "provides opportunities to help young people develop relationship and communication skills to help them *explore their own values*, goals, and options as well as the values of their families and communities" ("Curricula & Manuals," para. 6; italics added). Notice that school-based sex education is encouraging youth to *explore* their *own* values and the values of their families, not teaching them values. Teaching values is left for parents. Values and standards are an integral part of teaching children about sexuality. It's one thing to educate children on the specific mechanics of sex, but it's another thing to educate them on the reasons for sex and the context in which sex is appropriate. When discussing sexuality with your children, let them know what you feel and why you feel that way.

I gave an example earlier where a parent and child encounter teenagers kissing at the mall. There are specifics or facts a parent can give. It is usually something as simple as saying, "That's kissing." There is also a value placed on kissing. This is where we need to be careful: kissing is not bad in certain contexts. A lot of times parents want to hide their child from the inappropriate scene or say something that defines it as wrong. Children do not understand that when a parent says, "That's obscene," to a kissing teenage couple that it's only obscene in particular circumstances. You need to define exactly how you feel about kissing. Kissing is important to relationships. However, those relationships are more adult, more private, and more committed. When you say, "Kissing is important in a marriage or committed relationship, but it's not appropriate for two teenagers or in a place where there are lots of people," you send a few clear value messages. The first message is that kissing is good in a certain context, and you define that context as marriage or a committed relationship. Next, you define that teenagers should not engage in a particular type of kissing. Depending on the child's age, you can either simplify your language or include more detail. The last message is that kissing should be done in private. Both the specifics and the standards are laying the groundwork for teaching children what we expect of them later when it's time to start focusing on appropriate behavior.

Responsibility in Relationships

What is the purpose of sex in a marital relationship? It is to have children, yes? How many children do you have? How many times do you have sex with the sole purpose of creating a child? What happens when you are finished with your childbearing? Do you stop having sex? Many parents teach children about sex in the context of creating a child. This is good. However, there is more to sex than just creating a child. Your child needs to know that too. You don't need to disclose the details of how often you engage in sex or how good it feels to you, but children should be taught the relationship messages associated with sex. It's easy to think children already understand that sex has more place in a marriage than just creating babies. Or maybe you avoid talking about sex outside of creating babies because you are uncomfortable talking about those reasons. Many parents gloss over these positive intimacy messages and get right to the "don't do it until you're married" messages. Relationship messages are information about love, intimacy, respect, and communication within a union. Sex bonds a couple in ways that no other action of love can replace. Sex is for creating babies *and* for enjoyment and bonding in a marriage.

Relationship messages are ideas focused on intimacy, not just sex. *Sex* is the actual physical union of intercourse. *Intimacy* is sharing "close," "private," or "personal" information (*Webster's New World Dictionary*, 341). Intimacy is disclosing facts, feelings, experiences, and insights. Physical intimacy is generally known as sexual intercourse. However, there is also emotional, psychological, and social intimacy. When you teach children about intimacy in relationships, *all* aspects of intimacy, you are teaching them about relationships. Sex is just a part of true intimacy and oneness in marriage. Children need to be taught about the other reasons for sexual expression because they will be inundated with sexual images in society that have nothing to do with creating a child. Their lack of knowledge about positive intimacy from your perspective will be filled with the fictional Hollywood version of intimacy.

It is the "awareness of the beautiful power and positive commitment in the right kind of sex that gives children the best motivation and capacity to avoid what could hurt them and others" (Eyre and Eyre, *How to Talk to Your Child about Sex*, 16). Sex gives our marital relationship more intimacy. It connects a couple in a wonderful, beautiful union. Sex is an essential part of a healthy marital relationship. If you are not talking with your child about sexuality at all, they are not getting the positive relationship messages associated with sex. If you are only teaching your child that sex makes babies, they are not getting the positive relationship messages associated with sex.

Relationship messages include more than just explaining that sex is a great part of marriage, more than just creating babies. They include other ways to show love, such as writing letters, kissing, holding hands, performing service, and many other actions that express love. They include messages about ways to show love for *all* people through respect, like being friends with those who are different, not judging someone for differences in culture, and other ways to generally respect all of God's children. Relationship messages can also be broad and cover qualities that are desirable for any type of relationship, such as friends, brothers, sisters, grandparents, acquaintances, and spouses.

Ignoring relationship messages associated with sexuality can leave a gap in children's knowledge of appropriate sexual behavior. Children may hear details about sex from you or others. Then they may hear filthy or silly jargon and see unrealistic media portrayals of sexual behavior. If they only have details of sexual mechanics, they will be influenced by the feelings associated with the filthy or silly jargon and unrealistic media portrayals of sexual behavior. If you have started teaching them that sex is a positive, beautiful part of a committed relationship, they will see other sexual portrayals through lenses you have created. They will be more likely to filter out information that is contrary to what they have been taught by you. While they are young, they see you as knowing just about everything! This is a good time to capitalize on their adoration and teach them about the positive power of sexuality.

You can also be an example. Show children what good, responsible, loving parents look like. They learn a lot about intimacy, love, and respect by observing the way their parents interact with each other. Even if parents are divorced, the way one parent talks about the other parent or the way they support discipline and make decisions with the other parent teaches children about love and respect. You can add a comment occasionally to supplement what they see you do. For example, if you always kiss your spouse good-bye, you can occasionally tell your child why you do that. You may assume they know, but explaining behavior with words solidifies the act with the feelings of love. This combination creates a relationship message. A mother can say, "I like to kiss your Dad good-bye because I want him to know how much I love him and know that I think about him during the day."

Children learn that their bodies are special and should only be touched in special ways in a loving, committed relationship. They are taught that the commitment should be a marital relationship. They are taught that a significant other is not being respectful if they are not able to wait for the right context for sexual behavior and that it's not respectful for them to touch another person in sexual ways without their consent. They are also taught that sex enhances the quality of a beautiful, marital relationship. It is sacred, special, and feels good. Sexual behavior was created to feel good, and the desire to have sex is not immoral. Thoughts and actions surrounding sexual desire should be controlled, but the desire is good. That desire will lead to a fulfilling experience in a marital relationship.

I once met a woman who admitted that she cried after every sexual experience with her new husband for a few weeks after marriage. They had waited and controlled themselves before marriage, but she was so fraught with the negative messages of *don't, can't, sin,* and other ideas generally associated with chastity that she felt unclean, even though they had done everything right. She had obviously missed the positive messages associated with marital physical intimacy. Her parents were so focused on what *not* to do that they forgot to teach her the beauty and sacredness of positive sexual experiences in marriage. It is important to let your children know they need to "wait," but every discussion about sexuality should be filled with positive messages and good feelings.

When you discuss the temple with your child, what language do you use? Do you say, "Don't go there until you're older," or "Only sinful people can't go to the temple"? You don't use phrases like these because you want your child to look forward to attending the temple one day. You set their sights on the temple and use *encouraging* words. Usually, you use phrases like "You will be able to go to the temple someday," or "As you stay worthy you will be able to go inside one day." We look to the future and focus on what our children *will* experience in the beauty and sacredness of the temple. Children probably wouldn't care so much to attend the temple if we often used words like *don't, can't,* or *sin*. Similarly, as we focus on chastity with words like *don't, can't*, and *sin*, we are not setting on children's sights on the beauty and sacredness of their body and encouraging them to channel their energy into preparing for a proper time to benefit from sexual experiences in marriage. Sexual intercourse is an exquisite part of a marital relationship! Let your children look forward to it! They may be more likely to *want* to wait if they understand the positive power of sexuality in marriage.

Relationship messages are a good foundation for teaching your child the positive and pure meaning of sexuality. They are also a way to help your child understand the appropriate feelings associated with love, respect, and intimacy. This will aid your children in their dating years as they try to distinguish between proper feelings and behavior in relationships and inappropriate feelings and behavior.

4

Preparation

"Despair is most often the offspring of ill-preparedness."

—Don Williams Jr.

WHAT FOUNDATION is laid without adequate preparation? There is usually a plan or blueprint for guidance. Unfortunately, there is not a blueprint that will tell us exactly how to build the foundation for our children to have correct sexual knowledge, attitudes, and behavior. However, there is some guidance for how to plan effectively.

Plan Your Program

When a child comes to a parent with a question about sexuality, many parents start to panic. Why? Do you wonder if they're doing something inappropriate? Did someone do something to them that was inappropriate? What did they see or hear at school, at a friend's house, on television, or in any other setting? Maybe you wonder what you can do or say to prevent future uncomfortable sex questions. Most of all, do you feel unprepared? What can you tell your children that would be appropriate for their age? Is not knowing part of the panic?

One way to reduce the amount of times your child can surprise you with a question about sexuality is to be prepared. We are taught by our spiritual leaders to have food storage in preparation for an emergency and to save money in preparation for times of need (see *All Is Safely Gathered In*). We are also taught in the parable of the ten virgins to prepare ourselves spiritually (Matthew 25:1–13). Additionally, we are counseled to "prepare *every* needful thing" (D&C 88:119; italics added). We should prepare ourselves to answer our child's questions about sexuality.

How do we prepare? First and most important, spiritually prepare yourself so you can answer your child's questions with the right spirit. Sexuality was created by God for a specific purpose. There is a reason that fornication and adultery are listed as sins next to murder (Helaman 8:26). Both of these sins deal with things only God should control: giving and taking life. Most of us never consider taking away someone's life through our agency. However, there are many that, through this same agency, ignore the power of giving life.

You want to be sure your attitude, reactions, actions, responses, questions, discussions, and information are in accordance with the teachings of the gospel and the purpose of the body. Pray for guidance regularly, even if your child is not asking a question. Don't we prepare for an emergency before it happens, even if we aren't sure if or when it will happen? That's the meaning of preparation. Pray to be able to answer questions or see information about sexuality that your child needs addressed. Pray to have the Spirit witness to you when an ordinary question needs answered with special care. Pray to know what you should be praying for!

Next, realize that any disapproving emotional response you give usually trumps what you try to say. If disapproving feelings, an angry response (usually if the child uses bad language or has seen pornography), or the "sex is bad right now" attitude is taking over, set a time with your child to come back and answer her question later. Have you ever been in an argument or witnessed an argument where two individuals are yelling at each other? One starts yelling, so the second one yells louder to be heard over the first person. Then the first person starts yelling even louder to be heard over the second person, and so on. What do they remember from the exchange? Even if they remember the words, the emotional response is too potent to objectively understand the intended message. Try to practice managing your emotional response when an uncomfortable question is asked. You can practice with a spouse, parent, sibling, or friend. Have them ask you an uncomfortable question and practice responding. When the time comes that a child asks an uncomfortable question, you can at least think rationally before panic, fear, or another disapproving emotion can take over your response. Keep in mind that I used an example of anger and yelling, but *any* emotional response will overrun the intended message. This emotional response should be positive and spiritual. Then, even if your children don't exactly remember what you say, they will remember the Spirit and emotions they felt as being positive and good.

You can also ask your children questions before they ask. Parents may think they are protecting their child if they don't bring up sexuality before their child does. Some parents think if they talk to their child about sexuality, their child will be more likely to experiment. However, children with parents who talk to them about sexuality actually wait to have sex (see Karofsky, Zeng, and Kosorok, "Relationship between adolescent-parental communication").

There is logic for bringing up sexuality before your child does (as long as it is age appropriate). If you are asking the question, you have an answer already formulated. You have done your research and know what you should tell your child. You are also setting the stage for future conversations. In addition, some children never ask any questions. They may be afraid to ask questions. However, they still need the same information an inquisitive child obtains.

Children need facts in small doses. You can have a plan to bring up the subject of sex with your 7-year-old. First, you bring up that *sex* is a word she might have heard. You can ask, "Do you remember where babies come from?" This helps set up for a future discussion. At an appropriate time, you can ask, "Do you ever wonder how the baby gets in the uterus?" This brings a discussion about the mechanics of sex. This could easily be discussed over an age-appropriate children's book. Sometime later you can ask your child why people might have sex. Most children will think it's only to create a baby. You can reinforce the idea that it is for creating a child, but it is also a method of showing love for married adults. Sometime later you can ask your child to "read" the book you shared with them about sex or have him explain it to a favorite toy. This can reinforce what you have been teaching and give you a clue as to what information might need to be clarified. The great thing is that your child might get it and understand it with the correct information from you. Then you can breathe a sigh of relief for a while and start to plan your next move, answering his questions along the way.

When your child asks a question, plan your response. You may not know when the question will be asked or what it might entail, but you can plan. Here are a few ideas for general planning:

- Plan to answer honestly and clearly. Asking where babies come from is about the same as asking where the clouds come from. Children are curious about everything.
- Plan to ask your child a question or gain information before you begin to answer her question.
    - » Plan to ask clarifying questions. Usually your question or request will be for simple clarification. You may ask your child where she heard a term or explanation or what was happening when she heard it. You may ask what she thinks it is. You may ask what she saw that made her think to ask you such a great question. Sometimes children are asking for something different than you think. *Sex* can mean different things. For example, when a fill-in form asks for sex, it's asking whether you are physically a boy or a girl.
    - » You can plan to ask the child what he already knows about something so you can give him information he doesn't already know. You can say, "Tell me what you know about. . ." You could also say, "Can you tell me what you already know so I can answer with what you don't already know?

- Plan to say less rather than more. Children need to hear chunks of information. Give them a complete but simple answer. Once they understand that answer, they may come back with another question. If too much information is given at one time, your child may be easily confused and may mix up facts.
- Plan to postpone a discussion if the time is inappropriate. If your child asks you a question during dinner at a crowded restaurant, tell him that it's a great question but it's better to wait to answer it until you're done with dinner and around fewer people. Set a time with your child to come back and talk with him later. Only wait a few hours. Make sure you come back and talk with him later. If you don't, he will turn to other sources for the information. This information may be incorrect or lack the standard and sacredness you want to convey.
- Plan to *not* answer a question right away if you don't feel you can answer it correctly or adequately. Tell your child she has a good question and you're not sure how to explain it to her. You can say, "Great question. Can I think about that for a little while so I can give you a better answer?" Or you can say, "I'm not sure I have the right answer. Do you want to look it up with me?" I also enjoy asking my children if they want to find a book about it at the library. Look it up with or without them, depending on their answer, and discuss it. Also, if you feel you answered a question poorly, it is okay to go back and talk with the child again. You can correct misinformation or explain why you might have reacted in a particular way.
- Plan to repeat information. How often do children ask the same question? Usually, they ask a question multiple times. They also don't remember everything. Do you?

- Plan to *not* laugh at a child's question. Sometimes children ask questions we think are funny. Some of these questions involve sexuality. If the child is serious, we should also be serious. If we laugh at their questions, children are less likely to come to us with more questions. They are also more likely to feel ashamed, stupid, or embarrassed. Sexuality is sacred. Even if the question is funny, it deserves to be answered in the spirit of sacredness. For example, my friend recently spayed the family cat. Her 6-year-old asked, "Mom, when are you going to get fixed like the cat?" My first reaction when I heard this was to chuckle. However, this question was asked in seriousness. He thought that it must be normal for every female to get "fixed" when she is done having babies.

It may seem difficult to know when or how to start planning sexual education moments.

Certain times are perfect to begin talking about body parts with young children. These would be times when the child is naked for a few moments, like during bath time, diapering, dressing, and learning to use a toilet. There are often opportunities from television, other media, and friends where sexual expressions, behavior, or language can stimulate a discussion. You can ask your children what they think a certain word means, how they felt about what they saw and heard, what they think an interaction meant, and what they think you believe about certain behavior. This can also occur for other behavior, like serving others, being a good friend, and being kind and honest.

For older children, listen to what they are saying to their friends during carpools. Notice what billboards they see on a regular basis during routine driving. Watch their favorite shows with them a few times and take note of sexual behavior. Listen to their music. Read the books they are reading. Think about what questions you could ask them to stimulate a conversation. This is a good time to evaluate your attitude and standards. Later, when the time feels right, discuss with your children what they are seeing and what they think. This may be a time when you can have some new words defined for them or give your opinion and values about what they are seeing.

The advantage to this approach for older children is that you are trying to see the world from their perspective. You are also taking time to reflect on what your child is learning from the world and then waiting for a moment when it seems right to bring up a certain topic. For example, we lived in a city where two billboards on our regular driving route were very sexual. They made me uncomfortable. Our children were young, so a discussion about those billboards was never quite appropriate. However, if my children were older, I would have asked them how the billboard made them feel. What were they learning from the billboard? What was it even advertising? Why was it inappropriate? How did they teach us to view bodies or sex? What would their friends think about it? This can give you insights into how they believe their friends perceive sexual images or ideas.

Next, be prepared to listen. Communication is a vital component for knowing what to teach your child about sexuality. Effective communication includes the basics for any valuable conversation. Listening, using "I" messages, asking questions, and showing empathy are important components of effective communication. Be prepared to *not* assume you know what your child is thinking and feeling. Be prepared to *not* assume that a question from your teenager about sexuality means she is engaging in inappropriate behavior. Be prepared to deal with disagreements from teenagers. Be prepared to listen!

I was teaching a parenting class as a guest lecture once when a parent of young teenagers made the comment, "My kids don't argue with me because they know they'll get a long lecture. They hate lectures." She said this proudly, as if this was the biggest accomplishment she could have made as a parent! The goal of parenthood is not to have children who don't argue with you. Have you ever been wrong in your adult life? Have you ever been wrong as a parent? Teenagers are growing spiritually, intellectually, socially, and emotionally. It is great for them to disagree with something you say or do because this means they are thinking! The key is to disagree using effective communication. If you listen, you might learn how your child's world is making him feel, especially your tender youth.

We want to be heard so badly as parents that we often forget that the most effective part of communication is to really listen to our children. We want them to know how the world works and why it works the way it does. We want them to avoid making the same mistakes we made. We want them to have a better life than we had. We want them to be protected from the bad and experience the good in life. So we talk and talk. We tell them all the wisdom we have gained. We go on and on. We forget that children sometimes don't really want to hear what we have to say, have already learned something we are trying to tell them, or are not ready for it.

Be prepared to listen! Listen to what they are telling you. Listen to their body language. Listen to their tone of voice. Ask them, "How does that make you feel? Tell me what you think about that. Can you explain what you mean? What would you do in a situation like that? How would you react? What advice would you give your friends? What effect would that have on your reputation?" Don't turn every discussion into a mini lecture. Let them do the talking, and you do the listening.

It's important in planning to realize that once you talk about a sexual topic, it isn't going to go away. You can't breathe a sigh of relief and think, *It's over. I gave the big talk.* Even for older children, find ways to repeat information or have them tell you what they remember. They may put bits of information together to create an incorrect idea. When I was about eight, I thought that sex meant a man urinated in a woman's mouth. Some information I had was correct. Sex involved a man's penis and an opening from the woman. It took both a man and a woman. Something came out of the man and was received by the woman. However, the process was all wrong. My parents didn't define sex for me. I had probably received bits of information from my three older siblings that I formulated into a rather unpleasant idea.

Even when parents do explain sex and other sex-related topics, sometimes children mix up ideas and facts. Repetition until a child clearly understands and then an occasional refresher every so often will help your child retain correct sexual information.

The body is a temple. How often do children learn about the temple? They hear about it *at least* once a year during their Sunday school lessons at church. Once children learn a fact at school, is it never returned to the curriculum? No. Children hear things more than once at school. They even get to practice repeating information by doing homework and getting tested on their knowledge so the teacher can evaluate their understanding. Even at church, children are often asked to review what they know or to answer questions during a lesson. This is a way of testing their knowledge. Parents should also find appropriate times to have children review what they know about sexuality. It is not necessary or reasonable to question children too often about sexuality. They may only need a few discussions during a year. Usually a discussion is not a one-time lecture. Over the course of a few days, or a week or two, children have time to absorb new knowledge and can repeat it back correctly. During this time, you may have multiple discussions about a sexual topic. But you may only need to have these discussions two or three times a year. This is not a prescription for how often you should talk with your child. Take cues from your children and their environment. Whenever your children have questions, take time to answer them correctly.

How can you tell if what you're saying is getting across? Here are a few ideas for evaluating your children's understanding of what you have taught them:

- Ask your child how he would explain a sexual topic to a sibling, cousin, or friend. (You want to make sure you ask about a child in the age-appropriate group for this knowledge. Let your child know this information should be given by an adult, not a child.)
- Have your child draw a picture and explain it to you. (This would not be appropriate for the actual act of sex, but it would be appropriate for pregnancy, growth of a fetus, or ways to show love such as hugging and holding hands.)
- Ask your young child to "read" or tell you what pictures mean in a book about sex that you've been reading with her.

- Ask your child what the family believes about a sexual topic. Ask him why you believe that way.
- If you are pregnant, ask your child how the baby got in there. If someone else is pregnant, you can ask the same question, but it might be best to wait until it's just you and the child before you ask the question. You can also ask your child how the baby in your uterus eats, goes to the bathroom, grows, what it does, and other related questions.
- Ask your child to have one doll explain a sexual concept to another doll. You could also do this with trucks, puppets, toy animals, or other toys your child enjoys.

Keep in mind that other parents might not appreciate your child telling their child about sex. Let your child know that this is important information, but that it's the job of parents and adults to talk with children about sex. They should not repeat what they are learning to other children, but it is okay for them to come to you with any questions. Also, younger children in the family will learn the same information when they are ready. Let older children know that younger children are not ready for some information. It's just like waiting to be able to participate in other things because they are old enough, like a sleepover or riding a bike. Let your older children know that this information is not secret; younger children just aren't ready for more advanced knowledge when they haven't had the basics. For example, you are taught numbers before adding and adding before subtracting.

Your children do need someone to talk with about sex. Let it be you. Be prepared. Remember, your children may be hearing about sex. You may just not know about it and what bits they are learning. So you be the first word. Plan what you can teach your children and how to reinforce their learning so they can learn correct facts and standards.

SECTION 2

AGE-BY-AGE SEXUAL EDUCATION

Phase 1

Curious Learners

(Ages 0–5)

5

Love and Touch

"Each day of our lives we make deposits in the memory banks of our children."

—Charles R. Swindoll

As soon as your child entered this world, the first thing you wanted to do was hold that sweet baby. This was your child's first lesson in sexuality (remember, sexuality is not just sexual behavior; it includes attitudes and feelings about the body). Part of a healthy marital relationship is the ability to express love through physical affection. This is not only sex but also other gentle, desired physical affection. Babies and children want to be held. They are comforted by physical contact. When you provide the appropriate physical affection your children need, you are providing them with a reference for when they are mature and seeking to understand appropriate physical affection in their own committed relationships. You love your children, so you hold them, hug them, kiss them, and tickle them. When your children are older, they will understand that physical affection holds a special place in a loving relationship.

In providing appropriate physical affection for your children, listen to what they like and don't like. When you ignore your children's pleas to stop touching them in a particular way, you teach them that they don't have to listen to what other people desire in the physical aspect of a relationship. Or they may become confused about what they do like and don't like. For example, my son dislikes being tickled. This is difficult for me because I love to tickle him and to hear him laugh. I have found that there are times when he likes to be tickled, but I have to ask him first if it is okay with him if I tickle him. Often when I am tickling his little sister, who loves to be tickled again and again, he wants to join in the fun. He'll tell me where it is okay to tickle, usually his feet. However, he does enjoy having me run my hands through his hair. I have found this as a wonderful way to connect with him through touch. Some children may not like when you rub their arms or play with their hair. Pay attention to the kind of touch your children like and dislike and follow their lead. You are teaching them to be aware of their body and allowing them to have control over it. You are also teaching them how to respect other people's bodies by respecting theirs.

When your child is being touched by someone else in a way she doesn't like, encourage her to tell that person. For example, if my son was being tickled by a cousin or grandparent, I would encourage him to "use his words" and tell the person he doesn't like it. I would then try to make sure that the other person knows to honor that request. Children may just be children, but they know what they like and don't like. They don't have to be touched in a way they don't like, even if Grandma likes to pinch cheeks. If your child hates it, don't make him be subject to it. Encourage Grandma (or anyone else) to find another way to touch your child that he enjoys.

Touch is one part of teaching children about love. You can also teach children about love through language and example. You can describe what love feels like with words. You can say, "Love is a good feeling inside of you toward another person." You can describe love with many phrases, but it's best to use a simple one that they can easily understand. Children often want to marry their opposite-sex parent, an uncle or aunt, cousin, or even a sibling. One of my nieces adored my husband when we were engaged. She told her mom that she was going to marry him when she grew up. After we married, she staged a mock marriage with her and my husband. She loved my husband because he played with her and gave her attention. Her love was conditional on the time he spent playing with her. This is because children do not understand adult love. It's okay for children to love other adults and people in their lives. It's also important for them to understand the difference between family love and romantic love. If your children say they want to marry an adult or family member, you can say, "You love that person a lot. It's a great feeling to love a family member. Someday when you are older you'll find a great person that you will love in a different way and can marry. That person might be like (insert the name of the person the child mentioned)."

Children will also have crushes on other children. This is age appropriate. You don't need to discourage feelings of love or liking another person. These feelings are normal and pass quickly at this age. This is setting the stage for children to learn about the opposite sex. If there is inappropriate behavior, the behavior needs to be effectively handled. However, feelings at this age should be acknowledged, and you can ask your children why they like the other person. This helps them vocalize and realize what it is that they like about the opposite sex, again setting the stage and preparing the way for relationships in the future. If your child doesn't like to play with children of the opposite sex, find a way to encourage it. Children at this age like to play with same-sex friends. However, they learn more about the opposite sex and how to show respect for them by having opportunities to interact with them.

Children may also intrude on affection shown between parents or other adults they love. I was a nanny for one of my nieces when she was young. One time while my husband and I were engaged, she took his hand out of my hand and put it on his lap. She then took my hand and put it on my lap. She wedged herself between us and tried to get my attention. Moments like these are a good opportunity to tell your children that you love them very much. Explain that you can show love to both them and your spouse. Reassure them that you love them but can also love others. This may also occur when a new sibling arrives. Tell your children what you do to show them you love them. Also tell them what you do to show your spouse or other siblings you love them. Sometimes I involve my children in doing something nice for Daddy. I may let them help me cut out paper hearts and scatter them on the bed. This teaches them that love also has actions. It's not just a matter of the heart. Going on dates is another way to show your children that love has actions. Explain that you go on dates with Mommy or Daddy because you want to have special time together to learn more about each other. Church leaders have even stated that the relationship between a husband and wife is "more important than the parent-child relationship in teaching your children about intimacy" (*A Parent's Guide*, 24).

Love is what our society is using as a base for finding a marital partner. Children can learn through you how to give and show love. The way you show love to your children and others and the way you allow your child to show love shape your child's ideas about love and how it works. Children pick up a lot through observation but may not always realize that the acts of love that require work are showing love (doing a service for a spouse, like cleaning the bathroom). Showing love also needs to be defined through words. I have a friend who is frustrated with her husband at times because he thinks marriage should be easy since his parents never fought (or so he remembers). Love does require work and can be hard to define because everyone feels it differently. It's similar to feeling the Spirit. We can try to describe how it feels for us, but it may be different for someone else. Try your best to define love and how you show it to help your children understand that love requires work.

6

Self-Exploration

"To hear many religious people talk, one would think God created the torso, head, legs and arms, but the devil slapped on the genitals."

—Don Schrader

Years ago I was talking with a friend on the phone when her son started playing with his genitals. She stopped talking only long enough to disapprovingly say to him, "Stop touching yourself. Get your hand out of your pants." Then to me she said, "He's always touching himself. I can't get him to stop." This was said, as you can imagine, in a tone of voice that indicated he was doing something very wrong.

Beginning in infancy, children like to touch themselves. They touch their eyes, nose, ears, belly button, toes, and yes, penis and vulva. They love to explore their bodies. They want to know the purpose of all their body parts. They want to know what it feels like when they pull hair. They want to know what it feels like to put their finger in their nose or your nose. They want to know what it feels like to rub their penis or vulva. This kind of touching is just exploration. Children this young do not understand sex or masturbation in an adult way. They do not have the goal of sexual stimulation or orgasm. They just want to know what their bodies can do.

The nursery manual *Behold Your Little Ones*, for young children ages 18 months through 3 years, includes a lesson on bodies (40). An activity verse in this lesson encourages children to explore what their bodies are used for, such as eyes to see, hands to clap, and ears to hear. This lesson, like many others, teaches children to respect all parts of their body. When children touch their genitals and a parent responds in a disapproving way, children may learn that their genitals are dirty or bad. As children grow older, they may feel guilty about touching their genitals but will not learn the respect this area of their body requires for healthy sexual development. Genitals are wonderful organs and are part of our bodies for one of the highest purposes of mortality. Refrain from using a disapproving tone when referring to the genitals for any reason.

Negative reactions to a child's self-exploration may actually create an increase in the behavior because the child will focus on what you're telling them not to do. They do not always reason like adults. If you tell adults to stop reading, they may automatically start looking for something else to do. Young children do not often look for something else to do when you tell them to stop doing something. For example, when you tell toddlers to stop jumping on the couch, they often look at you and continue jumping. It is much more effective to redirect their attention and ask them to come read a book or play with a toy. When you say, "Couches are for sitting. You can jump on the trampoline," you are communicating with your children what they can do and what the expected behavior might be. This also applies to sexuality. If you give your children something else to do with their hands and not draw undue or negative attention to the behavior, you will find that most often they will not have a problem with continuously touching their genitals.

For infants, you can say, "Touching your body all over feels good." You can leave it at that and continue diapering, dressing, bathing, or whatever else it was that you were doing. For toddlers, you can say, "It feels good to touch yourself there, but it's not appropriate to do it where there are lots of people." For preschoolers, you can say, "I know it feels good to touch yourself in that way; these parts of your body are special and you are going to be able to use them in a special way when you are older." You may still need to reiterate that it is more appropriate in private. Then you can redirect their attention to another activity. You can suggest playing a game, reading a book, or having the children help with dinner. Boys will also quickly discover that when their penis is stimulated or they need to urinate, it will get bigger. For this scenario, it's best to say something similar to, "Sometimes your penis is small, and sometimes it gets bigger." There is no need for any other explanation for young boys. Just let them know it is normal for their penis to change size.

Approaching body exploration in this way allows children to explore and know their body. First, children learn their bodies and what they can do without feeling like their genitals are dirty. As they grow older, it teaches them that this kind of self-exploration is private, not public. Then you start teaching them that these parts of the body have a greater purpose for some time in the future. We are taught that "your reaction to these natural explorations will influence the way a child later feels about his procreative powers" (*A Parent's Guide*, 21). How do you want your children to feel about their ability to create new life?

Some self-touching is appropriate throughout life. Women and men are encouraged to perform breast or testicle self-exams. This is a form of exploration of the body. Keep that in mind when your toddler is rubbing his penis and discovers it can grow! Children don't generally masturbate until later in childhood (see Haffner, *From Diapers to Dating*). Masturbation is touching genitals with the purpose of sexual stimulation and orgasm. Young children are not generally engaging in sexual stimulation. And it is good for children to know their bodies. This way they can be aware of their body and any changes that may be good or bad, just like a breast or testicle self-exam.

For some children, self-exploration is a form of soothing themselves (see Haffner, *From Diapers to Dating*). If your children are often touching themselves when they are in new situations, around new people, or in environments that are over-stimulating, they might need some time away. You may also notice that your children often touch themselves during certain times of the day, such as bedtime.

If you notice that your children are regular in their time of self-exploration, you might consider creating a less stressful environment. You could also offer other items or behavior for comfort in stressful situations, like a hug or singing a favorite song.

Children do learn quickly that touching the genitals feels good. Isn't that part of their purpose? Weren't they created for this very thing? Your job is to help guide them in understanding when the genitals will be used for this purpose.

7

Privacy

"The child is curious. He wants to make sense out of things, find out how things work, gain competence and control over himself and his environment, and do what he can see other people doing."

—John Holt

The genitals were created by God, just as the eyes, ears, nose, and mouth were created by Him. Because the genitals are sacred, God has left it to parents to discuss details with their children. Children are taught in nursery, Primary, and young adult classes to respect their bodies. However, the details of sexual behavior are left to parents. This retains the privacy of sexual behavior and encourages it to remain sacred.

You can also reinforce the idea of privacy by teaching children that their genitals are their own, just like the rest of their body. They can tell other people what touch they want and don't want. Teach your children that certain people, like doctors and nurses, can touch their genitals and body because they are checking to make sure the child is healthy. Other people, such as caregivers, who help the child with regular washing also touch genitals during cleaning. Children can begin to clean their own genitals around preschool age. Teach them how to clean their genitals and encourage them to do it on their own.

Keep your own body private. However, it is not damaging for a very young child to see a parent naked. One seasoned parent describes motherhood as the inability to go to the bathroom alone. Another mother loves Saturdays because that is the day she can shower with the bathroom door locked. There are times as a parent that children may see you naked. That's okay for very young children. Parents should decide when they begin to feel uncomfortable having their child see them naked or their child gets silly or embarrassed about seeing a parent naked (see Haffner, *From Diapers to Dating*). If you aren't ready for questions about sanitary napkins or pubic hair, you may want to change your privacy needs.

This is also a guideline for bathing opposite-sex children together (see Haffner, *From Dating to Diapers*). It is fine for opposite-sex children to bathe together. However, when one child becomes self-conscious about it or the children get too silly about different body parts, it may be time to separate them during bath time. When you separate bath time, take care that you do not shame the children. If they are getting silly at bath time and you decide it is time to stop bathing them together, wait to discuss it with the children until another day. Explain to the older children that they are now big enough for a more grown-up way of bathing. They can start to bathe alone. If your children start touching each other in the tub (either opposite or same sex), calmly say, "Your penis (or vulva) is for you. It is special and sacred. Let's use our hands to wash our own bodies."

Clothing is also related to privacy. You can begin to connect clothing, privacy, and modesty with young children. Keep in mind that babies and young children have a more difficult time regulating their body temperature than adults. When clothing your children, look for signs of overheating. You can check by feeling ears or fingers to determine whether they are comfortably warm or too hot. You can also check by placing your palm on the child's back. Flushed cheeks may indicate overheating. If your child has sweaty skin or feels hot, clothing may need to be adjusted. My daughter has a much more severe reaction to heat than my son. If we are out in hot, humid weather for fifteen minutes, she gets a heat rash on her neck. I have to be careful to not only clothe her lightly in the summer but also keep her hair off her neck to reduce her core body temperature.

Parents make a personal choice based on their babies' signs of temperature in how to clothe them. Some parents may choose to put babies and toddlers in sleeveless shirts or tiny shorts to accommodate for temperature regulation. Some of these clothing styles are not appropriate for older children. As your child begins to regulate their temperature more adequately, you can begin to have simple discussions about appropriate clothes. For example, when buying a swimsuit for your 4- or 5-year-old child, you can explain why the two-piece suits are not appropriate. The clothing is there to give privacy and show respect for special body parts.

There are also other discretionary needs that teach children about privacy. Ask that your children knock before they come in your room, the bathroom, or any room with a closed door. Tell children when you need a minute to yourself; you need some privacy to pray or read scriptures. You may need privacy to make an important phone call or have a discussion with your spouse. In turn, respect your children's privacy. If they want some time alone, let them have it. If their door is shut, knock. Example is always an excellent teacher. To teach privacy, you must also give privacy.

8

Playing Doctor

"Whoever wants to understand much must play much."

—Gottfried Benn

It has been a great morning. You have done some laundry, dishes, and mopping. Your daughter has been playing quietly with her best friend, the neighbor boy. You decide to take a quick peep in her room before you throw a load of clothes in the dryer. You take a look around the door as you pass by the room and your mouth drops open. Your daughter is standing naked on the bed while the naked neighbor boy is standing on the floor, looking at her bottom with a magnifying glass. What do you do? If you are like many parents, you panic. Then you probably react.

Why do you react? You are reacting because you are worried the children are doing something that is disrespectful for their bodies and the other child's body. You are reacting because you worry that they are "having sex" or something similar that is not appropriate. You are reacting because you know that the body is a temple, sex is sacred, bodies are sacred, and your child and the other child are not respecting that sacredness.

Keep in mind that playing doctor can happen with both same-sex and opposite-sex children. Think like a child for a minute. Do preschool children know what sex is? They do not at this young age. Do preschool children know that looking at someone else naked is disrespectful? They might, but remember there are people, like doctors, looking at preschoolers' naked bodies and it is okay. When they think about respecting people's bodies, they are often thinking about concrete acts like hitting, pinching, or doing other similar unkind acts. Children this age are curious but physical in their thinking. When they are taught respect, it is mostly in the context of tangible things that harm others. They may not quite understand that the act of looking, which is a form of play for them, is disrespectful. Children may be able to recognize feelings that indicate what they are doing may be unwelcome behavior (which is why they close doors and get very quiet), but they may not be able to verbalize why they feel that way. Because they may not be able to form a concrete reason for why it is not welcome, they may still try out this type of play.

Children also don't connect nudity and sex. They are most likely not having sex or doing anything particularly harmful. This isn't behavior we want to continue, but the way you handle it may color their perception of sexuality. Your children will remember your reaction more than they remember what words you are saying. If you react by shaming the children or showing anger, they may remember the incident through shameful or angry lenses. If you react calmly with a reasonable explanation, the children will remember the lesson you are trying to teach them. The words you say probably remind them of the importance of privacy and bodies being temples. You also teach them about respecting other people's bodies. However, if they remember the negative reaction more than the words, what have you taught them? You were probably raging about good things, but they get lost in the emotional state. Think back to the basics for teaching children about sexuality. First, stay calm!

Next, calmly ask them to put their clothes on and come in another room. Ask it in a matter-of-fact way, as you would if you were asking them to start cleaning up. You can say something similar to, "It's time to put your clothes on and come in the living room."

You could also start with asking a question first to help give you time to calm down and feel in control of the situation. You could say, "What game are you playing? Let's put your clothes on and you can tell me about it into the living room." Asking the children to put their clothes on and come in another room gives you time to think and remain calm. When you react or use a disapproving tone of voice, this may convey to the children that they are in trouble. Their feelings of shame or fear of punishment may prevent them from understanding what you are about to explain to them. Other phrases you can say might include, "Wow, this looks like an interesting game. Let's put your clothes on and come into the living room so you can explain your game," or, "What game is this? You're both smiling, so it must be fun. It's time to put your clothes on and come into the kitchen."

Next, ask the children about the game they were playing. This is all they were doing—playing. Children are curious about other people's bodies. The body may be the same or different. Generally, their goal is not to harm one another but to engage in play. Children imitate what they see in the world around them. They are trying to understand and try out different roles from their world. Children are preparing for adulthood. They do this by trying on the roles of the adults in their life. For example, at the doctor's office, children take off their clothes to be examined by the doctor and nurse. They may take off partial clothing to be examined by a chiropractor. They try on these roles while they play, which may include some play where clothes are removed.

As you listen to their explanation of the game or play, you gain information about what kind of play was happening and the kind of explanation you should give. If they are playing a game similar to doctor, you can explain, "Doctors have you take clothes off so they can examine you. But when you play with a friend, your bodies are private and you should play these games with your clothes on." If they are playing a game mostly to see other children naked, explain that it is okay to be curious about other people's bodies but bodies are private. Tell them, "We need to respect other people's bodies and play with our clothes on." If children are curious about other children's bodies, you can read them books about the differences between boys and girls. Remind the children that their bodies belong to them and only certain people can look at and touch them.

You may want to ask the children some questions regarding consent (see Richardson and Schuster, *Everything You Never Wanted*). This is reinforcing the idea that your body is your own and you don't have to engage in any type of behavior in which you don't feel comfortable. You may need to wait to ask some questions until you are alone with your child. You can ask, "Was this game fun for you and your friend?"; "Did you and your friend want to play this game?"; "How did you feel during the game?"; "Did you or your friend want to stop after a little while, or did you both want to keep playing?"; "Will you let me know if this kind of playing happens and you didn't want to be part of it?" This is a precaution to make sure your child is not being forced to play this kind of game. However, if you shame your child or lecture when you find it happens, she is less likely to talk to you if it happens elsewhere and she *is* being forced to play.

Remember as you discuss this type of play with your child to keep your tone of voice in tune with a discussion (think of the temple while you are talking), not with a lecture or punishment. Children should not be punished for playing in this way. The behavior may then continue without your knowledge elsewhere or the child may feel shameful. Either of these responses from a child is not reaching the goal of teaching him that bodies are sacred temples and we respect all temples, every person's body. This kind of response also keeps those crucial communication lines open so you can talk with your child about sexuality in the future.

Last, let the parent of the other child know what happened (Haffner, *From Diapers to Dating*). Wouldn't you like to know if this happened with your child at someone else's home? Explain what you found to the other parent, away from the children. Include how you responded when you found them. After the explanation, you may want to say something similar to, "This is age-appropriate behavior. They weren't doing anything wrong. I am going to take a few precautions when my child plays with other children for now. I'm going to make sure all doors are open where they are playing. I'm going to check on them more regularly. I'll probably have a few more discussions on privacy and respect too." Make sure you allow your child to play with the other child again. They will know something is wrong if you ban them from playing with each other. They may begin to feel shameful or confused. If the other parent will not allow their child to play with yours again, find a truthful explanation that lets him know he isn't in trouble. Then suggest he call another friend he can play with.

If you are the parent getting the phone call, stay calm. Thank the other parent for letting you know. If you know the parent well enough, you could discuss ways to prevent it from happening again and coordinate your explanations so the children are getting the same information from you and the other parent. If your child tells you something happened at another child's house and the parent didn't tell you, thank the child for letting you know! Then you can talk with her about how she felt about it, what game it was, and if everyone wanted to play and discuss appropriate behavior. This may be a good teaching opportunity for helping her find words or ways to *not* do something she doesn't want to do when there are friends around. Dealing with peer pressure will be greater as children grow older. It would be wonderful for them to have some experience handling it while they are young.

Finding naked children playing a game can be disconcerting for a parent. You may fear many negative things are happening. In reality, most childhood games involving nudity are "I'll show you mine if you show me yours" games. Children are curious and want to see bodies. They want to know if they are the same or different. They are curious. Keep in mind that this is a good teaching moment to discuss what is appropriate or inappropriate and respectful or disrespectful. It may also provide you with some opportunities for giving your children tools to use when they don't want to engage in some type of play.

9

Questions, Answers, and Ideas

"A child can ask questions that a wise man cannot answer."
—Author Unknown

IF CHILDREN ARE old enough to start asking the questions, they are old enough to get straight, honest answers. These chapters with questions and answers are not designed to be a script for answering your child's questions or to fit all questions children may ask. This is a sample of questions your child might ask you about sex and some potential answers you can give. These sections are designed to give you a good reference if you panic when your child asks a question and you can't remember what to say. It is also designed to give you an idea of how you would frame an answer to a similar question. You need to think about and discuss these questions with your child's other parent(s) to decide how you might answer these or similar questions. Answers to these questions take prayer and spiritual guidance. This is just a starting point.

I have only given a few questions with answers. Your child may have many more questions not covered here. Answer them as immediately and as honestly as you are able. If you need a little time to find or articulate an answer, let your children know you will answer their question later. Then set a time to discuss the answer with them. In addition, some questions seem inappropriate for some children. Prayer should always be an integral part of answering your children's questions and knowing which sexuality topics to discuss and when to discuss them. We don't *want* to have to discuss some of these topics with children, but because of the world they live in, we *need* to address topics when they arise. Otherwise they will be learning what the world wants them to learn.

Remember to refer to the basics when answering a question. Acknowledge that the children are asking a good question. You can use phrases like, "Good question," "Great question," "I'm glad you asked," "What a thoughtful question," and "That is an interesting question." Then clarify the question. Make sure you know what your child is really asking. Remember, it is best to give a simple, one- or two-sentence explanation. The children may then ask a question that would require another answer. However, if your children don't ask another question, you can give them time to absorb your answer before giving them more information. You can also find ways to continue reinforcing knowledge they have gained.

It is also important to remember that sex is not all about physical expression. It is about the ultimate relationship: marriage. Connect sex as a form of reproduction and part of a healthy way to express love in marriage. Friendships are increasingly important as children mature. You can use your discussions about friendship as a reference for respect, which is critical in a sexual relationship. Children should begin practicing respect in their friendships. This will guide them in their future mature relationships. If they understand and practice respect in their friendships, this will transform into respect for a sexual marital partner.

Value statements are included with some answers. These values may not reflect your own. They are a reminder that there is a value lesson to be learned and you should be teaching that to your children, along with the facts. If a value stated here is not a family value for you, insert your own value as you teach your child. There are also a few ideas for starting a conversation about sexuality with a child in this age group.

Question and Answer

Q: Where do babies come from?

A: Babies grow in a special place in a woman called a uterus. It's close to the stomach.

V: Having a baby is special. It makes a family grow. Heavenly Father wants us to have families.

Q: Can I have a baby?

A: (Boys) Only women have uteruses, so only women have babies. However, men have a special role in getting a baby started. (Girls) When you get bigger, your body will change a little so you can have a baby too.

V: Having babies is for families with a married man and woman. When you get married, you can choose to have a baby.

Q: How does the baby get in the uterus?

A: A man and a woman are needed to start a baby. Inside the woman are tiny eggs. Inside the man are tiny sperm. When an egg and a sperm meet, they can start a baby.

V: A man and woman should be married to have a baby.

Q: What is sex?

A: (Hopefully, they're not asking this yet. But if they do, remember to clarify and ask what they know because another child may have told them something, and you might have to give more information than you generally would at this age.) When two grown-ups love each other, they like to kiss, hug, and touch in a special way that feels good.

V: This is for a married man and woman who love each other.

Q: How does the baby get out? Or how will the baby be born?

A: The baby will come out of a special place called the birth canal. It's an opening between a woman's legs called the vagina.

V: Heavenly Father has made special body parts for this wonderful experience.

Q: Does it hurt when the baby comes out?

A: It does hurt some when the baby comes out because the

opening is stretching to let the baby come through a small opening. It's like pulling your hand out from between the bars on the kitchen chairs (or something similar). It squeezes a bit.

V: Even if it hurts, babies are so special that some hurting for the baby to come out doesn't bother me.

Q: Can I see where the baby comes out?

A: It's in a special place that is private, so I prefer not to show you.

V: These places are so special they need to stay private, except for certain times, like having a baby.

Q: Why does my penis get big and hard?

A: Sometimes it is big and hard and sometimes it is small and soft. They just do that. It is part of the way they work. **For parents**: penises harden about every ninety minutes for young boys because of contact or the need to go to the bathroom (Haffner, *From Diapers to Dating*, 39).

Q: What happened to my penis (as in, I don't have one and someone else does)? Or what is that (referring to a penis or vulva)?

A: There are special parts for boys and special parts for girls. Boys have a penis and girls have a vulva. You are a girl (or boy), so you have a vulva (or penis).

V: Boys and girls have different parts, but they are both equally special.

Q: Why does he stand to pee and I sit (or vice versa)?

A: It is easier for a girl to sit to pee because her opening is near the vagina. It is easier for a boy to pee standing up because his opening is on his penis.

Ideas for Conversation Starters

- Show pictures of you pregnant with your child. Show pictures of your child as a newborn. Ask some questions about where babies might come from.
- Read books about where babies come from (see the list of additional resources).

- During bath time, label all the parts of your child's body, including genitals.
- Ask your preschooler, "What is the difference between boys and girls?"
- If you are pregnant, ask your child about what the baby does, how it grows, how it goes to the bathroom, and how it eats. If someone else is pregnant, you can ask the same questions, but it might be best to wait until it's just you and the child before you ask questions.
- Ask your child, "What would you do if someone was touching you in a way you didn't like? What if that person didn't stop when you told them to?"
- Ask your child, "What would you do if someone told you to stop touching him in a certain way?"
- Ask your child, "What is your favorite way to be touched?"
- Ask your child, "What does love feel like to you? What does love look like? What do you love?"
- Ask your child, "How can you be a good friend? Who is a good friend to you? Why?"

Phase 2
Concrete Learners
(Ages 6–8 and 9–11)

10

Ages 6–8: Peers

"I like her because she smiles at me and means it."

—Author Unknown

As children grow older and begin school, friends become an important part of their world. Most children begin to outgrow playing doctor, although some children may still engage in it during these ages. Their new play creates new challenges for parents. Are sleepovers okay in our increasingly sexualized world? What do I do when my child tells me they have a boyfriend or girlfriend at this age?

"Mom, can I go, please, please, please, please?" Sleepovers are an intensely fun idea for children in the early school-age years. When your children beg you to sleep over at a friend's house, you may be wondering many things: Will they be safe? What movies will the other parents let them watch? What values are taught in the home? Will it be an all-girl or all-boy party? Will your child actually be fine without you for one night? Will there be any possibility for your child to be molested? Will there be alcohol in the home that needs to be in a locked cupboard?

Some of these questions you may not ask because you know the friend's parents well. However, as your children have more friends, it's more difficult to know all of their friends' parents well. A simple phone call can ease the worries of mixed-sex sleepovers and what movies or activities are planned for the night. Safety and values may be more difficult to determine if you don't know the parents well. You can ask to meet the parents before the sleepover or just speak to the parents on the phone. You don't want a conversation to turn into a grilling session of the other parents, but there are some safety and value concerns that you may want to address. You may ask if there is alcohol in the home and how the parents protect the children from it. You can ask what kind of movies they allow their children to watch and where they keep the more adult movies. Most parents will be glad you are concerned for your child's safety, as long as you are gentle and have a short list. If you have an overly long list of things you are concerned about, the other parent may feel you are judging them. Try to keep in mind that the big things are the really important ones, like if the children have access to alcohol.

The question of "Will there be any possibility for my child to be molested?" weighs heavily on some parents' minds for certain sleepovers. If you don't know the parents well, you are more likely to ask this question. However, most children are molested by someone they know (see Finkelhor, "Current Information on the Scope and Nature of Child Sexual Abuse"). Your child is more at risk of molestation by those in your own family than their friend's family. This does not mean there is no risk. There is still a small risk. Check websites for sex offenders in the area you live and where your children are spending time with friends. The website http://www.familywatchdog.us/ is a national registry for sex offenders. Do your homework before you send your child to a sleepover. However, keep in mind that your child may be more at risk of sexual abuse at a big family reunion than at a sleepover.

Some parents keep their children home from sleepovers because the fear of molestation is greater than the faith they have that as they do their best to keep their children safe, the Lord will guide them. Pray for guidance to know if your children should not be sent to a particular home for a sleepover if you feel uncomfortable. If you have been teaching your children that they have a right to say no to *any* touch they don't like, then you just need to remind them of this as they skip off to the sleepover. You don't want to scare them and make them think someone might touch them in a way they don't like. This may actually create a problem. They may be more worried and wary of people. They may interpret positive touch, like a loving hug from a friend's parent, in a negative way. You can say, "With a lot of kids and adults around, you might have some kids or adults touch you in a way you don't like. Maybe they will tickle you too much. Remember you can just tell them to stop. If they don't stop, find another adult or person to help you. If someone tells you to stop, remember to listen to their words." This is a simple reminder of respecting others and their bodies, along with expecting respect for their own bodies. You can also add that if there is any touch they feel uncomfortable with, even if they've never been touched that way before, they can tell the person to stop.

You can also remind your children that if anything feels uncomfortable for them, a movie, type of play, picture, or other activity, they can speak up and say they don't want to play or get involved. If your children get too uncomfortable, they can always call home and have you pick them up. Let them know uncomfortable feelings can be the Spirit's way of telling them they shouldn't do something.

Another concern as peers become more important to your children is the possibility of boyfriends or girlfriends. *For the Strength of Youth* guides children to not date until they are 16 years old. This is wise counsel. However, some of you may think this applies to "boyfriends" and "girlfriends" when your children are 6, 7, or 8 years old. You may discourage your child from having a boyfriend or girlfriend because of this counsel. Dating is having "romantic social engagement[s]" (*Webster's New World Dictionary*, 168). Children this young are not engaging in romantic social events with another person. They just like someone a great deal, and the other child usually doesn't know or return the feelings. My 4-year-old son told me he had a girlfriend one day. I asked him what that meant. He said, "You know, she's my friend and she's a girl. I'm her boyfriend." This is a good teaching moment. Ask your child why he likes the other child. This can be a foundation for learning about love and friendships. You can teach him to be respectful and kind to children of the opposite sex, but encourage him to think about why he likes other children too. This is reminding him that he can have different feelings for different friends without encouraging him to have feelings for only one other child.

Some children have very special friends that they treat differently than other friends. They may hold hands with these friends or put their arm around them. As long as both children are happy with these touches, there is no reason to discourage this kind of behavior. In fact, it might be important for learning about how to treat the opposite sex. Kissing games, like kissing tag, when children are young are also not inappropriate. The kissing is usually on the cheek and devoid of sexual meaning. If you feel uncomfortable, you can gently suggest another game to play.

Another issue that arises when your children are more engaged with peers is pornography. Children are being exposed to pornography at very young ages. I had a wonderful stake president who informed me that he didn't realize how young this could occur. He had to combat pornography with his ten-year-old son, who had been exposed to it for a couple of years by the time he found out. Children need to be taught what pornography looks like, what to do if they come across it, and how to repent and ask for help when they've been exposed to it. As a beginning for teaching our son (though daughters need to be taught as well), we taught him what to do if a picture popped up on the computer that made him uncomfortable. We discussed what type of clothing is appropriate. When we saw a picture of someone in an inappropriate bathing suit or clothing, we asked him how he felt, what he should do, and why it wasn't okay to look at the picture. One day, we were watching a YouTube video. An advertisement on the side had a picture of the top of someone's naked backside. He seemed drawn to it, and I asked, "Is that interesting to look at?" He said, "Yes." I said, "I know it's interesting to look at other people's bodies. Is it appropriate?" He said, "No." I asked him why it was inappropriate and what he should do. He had already averted his gaze as the discussion began, knowing that was the right thing to do. He was 6 years old at the time. He didn't realize he was having a lesson in pornography. It starts simple. As children mature, you need to address not only clothing but also behavior and language. As you encourage children to have respect for other people's bodies through modesty in clothing, behavior, and language, they will be less likely to get involved in pornography.

As peers become more important to children, you may find you have some significant moments where you can teach them about sexuality. They learn about respecting other people's bodies, listening to other people's likes and dislikes, knowing their own likes and dislikes, and understanding feelings of love and like, to name a few. You will have more opportunities to discuss privacy, clothing, modesty, and pornography. You will also have more moments for teaching children about feeling the Spirit, which will become increasingly important as they mature.

11

Ages 6–8: Masturbation

"A child educated only at school is an uneducated child."

—George Santayana

Children learn so many things at school we wish they wouldn't learn or wish they would learn a little older. Many of the things they learn are grotesque or distorted images of sexuality. Masturbation is one of these sexuality issues. Children will hear people talk about masturbation or may even see someone masturbating. The world's view on masturbation tends to be favorable. In fact, some encourage it as a healthy and safe way to relieve sexual pressure (see Levkoff, "She-bop & He-bop"). These proponents argue that it is a way for children, young adults, and single adults to relieve this sexual pressure without the potential negative effects of pregnancy or sexually transmitted diseases. Not only that, but they also argue that individuals should masturbate to learn what they like sexually so they can communicate that with a partner. However, we believe it is debilitating for our spirits (see "Talking with Your Children").

We have already established that young children do not masturbate but self-explore. Sometime before or during puberty, self-exploration can become more deliberate, with the intent of creating sexual stimulation. Not all children will self-explore or masturbate. If you find your children touching their bodies in this way, you need the guidance of the Spirit before beginning a conversation with them about masturbation. In the moment, keep your language to your children simple and direct. You could say, "I know it feels good to touch your body that way, but there is a time for this kind of touching and now is not the time. Please find something else to do with your hands." Later, after you have had a chance to prepare yourself spiritually for this kind of discussion, find a private place to talk with your children.

The most critical beginning to this discussion should be a reminder that the children's bodies are temples. Their bodies are beautiful, wonderful structures that should be treated with care. Just as the temple should be treated in a special way, the body is also treated in a special way. We wear special clothes in the temple to signify purity. We wear clothes over our bodies to cover special places and keep sacred places holy and pure. We do not use certain language or behavior in the temple, like running and yelling, to keep the temple clean and pure. Our bodies also have certain limitations to keep them pure and clean. One of these limitations is to wait for sexual touches until the proper time and place. Explain that these parts of the body are made for feeling good. But just as your body, heart (desire and will to learn correctly), and mind have to be ready before you can walk, run, or ride a bicycle, your body, heart (spirit), and mind also have to be ready for sexual excitement before it should be used that way. There is a time that your body, spirit, and mind are ready for sexual experiences. That time is in marriage.

You may want to let your children absorb this knowledge before you begin your next explanation associated with masturbation. Self-stimulation with the goal of sexual excitement is selfish. The main goal of masturbation is to please oneself. Generally, there is nothing in it for anyone else. However, one reason our bodies were created is to enjoy sexual expression in becoming one *with someone else.* The genitals were created for pleasure but with appropriate conditions. Just as we have to do certain things to be worthy to enter a temple, like paying tithing and having faith, we also have certain things we do before we are worthy to exercise our body in a sexual way. We find a partner we love and cherish and get married. Then we are worthy to righteously use our body in a sexual way. Sexual expression is about a couple, while masturbation is about a person.

The last thing you may want to discuss with your children is what to do if they do masturbate. There may be times when they do it without thinking. It is a process for them to move from self-exploration to masturbation. Let your children know that as soon as they realize they are touching their bodies in this way, they should stop. Encourage them to find something else to do. Let them know that everyone makes mistakes and reassure them that Heavenly Father loves them and that you love them.

If your children masturbate, you don't want them to feel so guilty about the behavior that they can't think of anything else, thus making the problem worse. Give them the information they need to know and be guided by the Spirit. Be careful in your reaction if you find your children masturbating after you have had a discussion with them. Reacting instead of acting may create guilt rather than desire to change. Guilt, or feeling sorry, is an essential part of repenting, but it isn't the main ingredient. Repentance is "motivated by love for God and the sincere desire to obey His commandments" (*True to the Faith*, 132).

Even if your children never masturbate or have long ago left self-exploration behind, masturbation should be on your list of topics to discuss around puberty (see "Talking with Your Children"). It is pervasive in our society. A discussion of what masturbation is and why we reserve any sexual stimulation for marriage is important for youth. They will view future discussions about masturbation at school, friend's houses, workplaces, and other settings through the lens of the purpose of sexuality. The pleasure associated with sexuality is a joint, marital experience. They will see sexuality as a sacred, beautiful experience they will want to share with a marital partner.

12

Ages 6–8: Sex

"Some parents feel embarrassed to speak frankly to their children about sexual intimacy. However, the world is not embarrassed."

—from "Talking with Your Children about Moral Purity"

One of my friend's children came home from kindergarten and asked her, "Mom, what's sex?" He was only six years old at the time. My friend, of course, had a moment of panic. This was her oldest child, and the topic was not on her to-do list. She told him it was a special snuggle for moms and dads. Since she had given him an answer, she was not ready or eager for him to bring it up again. The case was closed.

I hope you realize that the case is not closed. If you are not teaching your child about sex, who is? Who do you *want* to teach your child about sex? What terms do you want your child to associate with sex? Children this age are much more interested in how the sperm and egg get together. However, the ideas they get from other people may create confusion. Children may get pieces of the truth. However, without having them connected in the correct way, children may create fantastic ideas surrounding sex. Some children may worry that they can get pregnant from being in a bathtub or swimming pool with another child, whether male or female. I mentioned that as a child I believed sex was when a man urinated in a woman's mouth. What do you want your children to believe?

You are your children's best teacher. When you explain how the sperm and egg get together, you know they are learning correct information. You also know, by having them repeat what you are teaching them or by comments they make, what information they are misunderstanding. Children need things repeated! You then have the opportunity to correct any misunderstandings. After an explanation of sexual intercourse, my friend's 7-year-old son exclaimed, "You mean a man just pops off his penis and shoves it in a woman?" He had misunderstood a concept. Penises do not come off during sexual intercourse. His mom asked, "Does your penis come off?" She was then able to correct a misconception. If he had heard about sex from a friend, there may have been this or other misconceptions that would have continued in his sex education.

Children, learning from you, will be able to see, hear, and understand sex through the lens you desire. The lens you are trying to shape has the focal point on the temple. The temple is not just the place where they will go someday to get married but a sacred and holy place. Likewise, the body is a temple and should be treated with respect. They will see that sex is good under certain conditions. They will see other slang terms as incorrect and distasteful. They will develop the attitude about sex you are creating for them. Isn't it important that children should learn about sex when you, the parent, are still seen as Mr. or Mrs. Know-It-All? They believe you more than any other person at this age.

Think back to your experiences learning about sex. Who told you about sex? How old were you? What were you told? What do you think was a positive experience in shaping your sexual attitudes? How can you create those positive experiences for your child? A man I know remembers a "birds and the bees" talk when he was about 9 years old, although he can't remember any details. He doesn't remember another conversation or discussion until the morning he was married. On the way to the temple, his father gave him a bottle of lubricant and told him he might need it. There was a sixteen-year gap between the "birds and the bees" talk and the wedding night! Everything he learned in the middle was given to him by peers, the media, and crude jokes.

Values are also an important component of any explanation surrounding sex. What does your family value? As members of The Church of Jesus Christ of Latter-day Saints, we value sex within a marital relationship. We value sex as a pleasurable expression of love. We value sex as an opportunity to create a child. We value sex as an opportunity for oneness in a marriage. Children are often told the mechanics of sexual expression. Teens are often told to not have sex until they are married. Make sure you are not missing the relationship component. The relationship component is not just waiting until marriage. Sexual expression is to create a bond between a husband and wife. It is an expression of love, respect, and passion. Let your children know what sex does for a good marriage. Sex can make a good marriage better! You don't have to be detailed, especially about your relationship with their other parent. But explain to them what sex means to a marriage and a relationship.

Elementary aged school children often talk about the opposite sex having "cooties." When you explain the mechanics of sex to children this age, the typical response is "yuck," "gross," or some other similar exclamation. One 7-year-old I know exclaimed, "That is so inappropriate." Isn't it interesting that children should learn about sex when it still seems "gross" and their hormones haven't kicked in yet? It's a normal reaction for children to feel this way. You can say, "It is okay to feel that way. I can see how it might sound gross now. When you are older you might find you feel differently." If you think about the concept of sex through a child's eyes, it does sound gross. They still think by touching the opposite sex they might get cooties!

As children grow older, they are less likely to be open to conversations regarding sex. It does become uncomfortable. But it is more uncomfortable if there haven't been any previous conversations. I've mentioned my friend whose dad gave him and his brother a sex talk when they were about 12 and 9. He was the oldest. He said he was very uncomfortable with the conversation and tried to think of a way out of it, but his younger brother was fascinated by the discussion. His brother was open to asking questions and repeating what he'd heard. My friend said he did want to know but wished his brother would stop asking questions because it was just uncomfortable. He also had questions he wanted to ask but was too uncomfortable. If his father had waited another two years, my friend may not have been open to even participating in the discussion! Teens may say they already know about sex to avoid having an uncomfortable conversation, or they may believe what their peers are telling them. However, they often don't know the correct information, only partially know the correct information, or know only the rumors their friends have been telling them. Again, isn't it important that children should learn about sex when they are still willing to listen to you?

Parents may worry about the timing and amount of information to tell children regarding sex. It is important to refrain from telling children too much at too young an age. But if you wait too long or tell them too little, they may be incorrectly or negatively informed. Children should be told about sex by the time they are 8 years old (see Richardson and Schuster, *Everything You Never Wanted*). Children are baptized at age eight. We are taught that children are baptized at age 8 because before this time they are "innocent" (Packer, "Children," para. 24). Innocent means children are "free from sin" and do not *know* evil (*Webster's New World Dictionary*, 334). President Eyring further explains, "The family has an advantage in the first eight years of a child's life. In those protected years, because of the Atonement of Jesus Christ, Satan's use of the mists of darkness to hide the path to return home is blocked" ("Help Them on Their Way Home," 23). Isn't it important that children should learn about sex when they are still innocent and Satan does not have power to cloud their judgment? They may still have some incorrect ideas and make mistakes, but when you teach them the things of Christ, that is what they are naturally drawn to and feel is right. This is the time to teach them righteousness and morality and expect them to live it (see *A Parent's Guide*). These teachings will stay with them in later years.

Children from ages 6 to 8 are also interested, honest, and factual. They are not embarrassed, cynical, sarcastic, and unapproachable. They should learn the facts and beauty of sexual expression before Satan can pollute their ideas. They will carry this with them while they grow older. Even when they learn some of the base ideas of a sexualized world, they will still have had the correct teaching and attitude instilled in them during the most influential time of their life.

13

Ages 6–8: Questions, Answers, and Ideas

"You know children are growing up when they start asking questions that have answers."

—John J. Plomp

Question and Answer

Q: What is masturbation?

A: This is when people touch their own genitals (you can say penis, vagina, or clitoris) to get special tingly, exciting feelings. This is different than touching your genitals for cleaning or wiping after going to the bathroom.

V: Masturbation is something other people might do for pleasure. It doesn't hurt your body, but it is not good for your spirit, just as saying bad words doesn't hurt your mouth, but it hurts your spirit. You should wait until you are married for those special tingly, excited feelings.

Q: What is sex?

A: Sex is when a man and a woman get very close and place a man's penis in the woman's vagina.

V: A man and woman should be married to have sex. It's a beautiful part of their marriage. It brings them closer and is a way they show they love each other. It's also a way to create a child.

V: Both a man and a woman should want to have sex. One person should not try to force or convince the other person to have sex. If someone tries to force you or convince you to have sex, you should tell Mom, Dad, or another trusted adult.

Q: What are my private parts?

A: Your private parts include all of your genital area (penis or vulva), buttocks, and as girls grow older, their chest and breasts.

V: Your private parts are sacred and are used for a wonderful purpose in the future. If someone tries to touch any of these parts, you can tell that person to stop. You should tell Mom, Dad, or another trusted adult if this happens. We want to help you keep your body sacred. If someone does touch your genitals, it is not your fault. Even if you feel bad, Mom, Dad, or another trusted adult need to know. We will not be angry with you (and don't get upset in front of the child, even if you aren't upset at them!).

Q: Does sex hurt?

A: Sex shouldn't hurt. It is a pleasurable, enjoyable experience for a husband and wife.

V: Sex should be enjoyed only between a married man and woman.

Q: What is an erection?

A: It is when extra blood goes into your penis and it gets big and hard.

Q: Why do people who are not married have sex?

A: Some people do not believe what we do. Sexual feelings, called sexual desire, are powerful when you get older, and some people think it is too hard to wait until marriage.

Some people believe it is a way of showing love that is appropriate if the relationship is committed in some way.

V: We should love all people, regardless of their choices. We believe in our family that the best choice is to wait until you are married to have sex. That is when you are mature enough to handle the responsibility and beauty of a sexual relationship. You can control sexual desire. It may not be easy, but it will be worth the wait.

Q: How do the sperm and egg meet to make a baby? (This is the next level for answering where a baby comes from. First, it was just a sperm and egg meet.)

A: When a man and a woman have sex, the penis goes in the woman's vagina. The penis releases sperm into the woman's vagina. The woman's body releases an egg. Then the sperm and egg can meet to make a baby.

V: The man and woman should be married to have sex and make a baby. This feels good to them and is a great part of marriage.

V: Sex is for making babies and for enjoyment for the man and woman. It brings them closer together and is a good thing for their marriage. It's a way for them to show they love each other.

Q: When does the sperm know it's time to come out?

A: It's like when you need to pee. Your penis feels like it's time for the pee to come out. That's kind of what it feels like when it's time for the sperm to come out. The penis feels like it's time to let the sperm out.

Q: Can you use up all your sperm?

A: No. Your body makes sperm all the time. After some comes out, the body starts to make more and store it until the next time you use it.

Q: Can you use up all your eggs?

A: A woman's body has a certain number of eggs. But there are enough eggs for most women to have lots of babies.

Q: What is sexy?

A: It is a way adults describe someone else they find attractive or like the way that person looks.

V: This is an adult word to describe another adult because it is associated with strong romantic feelings, or adult love. It is not an appropriate way for children to describe themselves or others.

Q: What are pads, tampons, or sanitary napkins?

A: Women have a uterus to help a baby grow. The uterus is a special place that protects the baby. Every month, a woman's body prepares the uterus for a baby. If a baby is not created, or the sperm and egg don't meet, the body cleans out the uterus and starts again. The lining of the uterus, which is like blood, slips out through the birth canal, or vagina. It can be a little messy, so women use pads, tampons, or sanitary napkins to keep their clothes clean during those few days. (This can be a little too much for some young children. Simplify it for younger children).

V: It can be a little messy, but it's an amazing process that Heavenly Father gave women that can help a baby grow.

Q: What are you doing? (Your child has just walked in on you during sex.)

A: "Please go back to your room. Your father (mother) or I will be there in a minute." (You may be embarrassed, but try to say this matter-of-factly and with love.) Put some clothes on. "What did you see?" Wait for an answer and then respond to it. "What do you think was happening?" Wait for an answer and then respond to it. Answer them briefly but honestly. You don't have to go into the details of sex. Reassure them if they were worried.

V: Let them know that one way adults show they love each other is to touch each other in a special way. This is for married adults. Remind them of privacy. When a door is shut, that means you want some privacy. They should knock and wait for an answer before walking in a room.

Ideas for Conversation Starters

(Duplicates from previous chapters and age groups are conversations that should still be happening at this age, because it is important to repeat information that has previously been discussed).

- Read books about how babies are made (see the list of additional resources).
- Read books about how babies grow in the uterus.
- Read books about sexual expression. Read books that include the mechanics of sex and books that include the importance of love in the relationship.
- Ask your children, "What do you remember about where babies come from, how a baby grows, why people have sex or sexual intercourse, who should have sex?" and anything else you have already taught them. Remember, they need to hear things more than once, just like you.
- Ask your children how they would explain a sexual topic to their younger sibling, cousin, or friend. Remind them that they shouldn't share this information with younger children because they aren't ready yet, but you just want to see if they understand what you've taught them.
- Have your children draw a picture and explain it to you. This is probably more appropriate for concepts surrounding babies growing in the uterus, birth, and those kinds of topics. It is probably not appropriate to have your children draw someone engaging in sex.
- Ask young children to "read" or tell you what pictures mean in a book about sex that you've been reading with them. Or you can have older children summarize a book you have read.
- Ask your children what the family believes about a sexual topic. Ask them why you believe that way.
- If you are pregnant, ask your child how the baby got in there. If someone else is pregnant, you can ask the same

question, but it might be best to wait until it's just you and the child before you ask the question. You can also ask your child how the baby in your uterus eats, goes to the bathroom, grows, what it does, and other related questions.

- Ask your child to have one toy explain a sexual concept to another toy. You could do this with trucks, puppets, toy animals, or other toys your child enjoys.
- Ask your child, "What would you do if someone was touching you in a way you didn't like? What if she didn't stop when you told her to?"
- Ask your child, "What would you do if someone told you to stop touching him in a certain way?"
- Ask your child, "What is your favorite way to be touched?"
- Ask your child, "What does love feel like to you? What does love look like? What do you love? Who do you love?"

14

Ages 9–11: Puberty

"The best way to keep children at home is to make the home atmosphere pleasant, and let the air out of the tires."

—Dorothy Parker

The school system is generally teaching puberty around fifth and sixth grade. This may vary according to state or school district. Some may teach it once in both grades. Some may teach it at a younger grade. However, the school system is not designed for your specific child. Children begin puberty when their bodies are ready. The school system should really only be a support for what you are teaching your children at home. It is important to know the curriculum your children are being taught at school. You can supplement what they are learning with your family values. You can also reinforce what they are learning by asking questions.

In addition, if something being taught in school is not in harmony with your family values, you can make a decision about what you want your child to learn from the school and when you might want to keep them home. Keep in mind that even if you keep your children home from a school sexuality lesson, they will hear what was taught by other children in their class. If you are keeping them home because you don't think they should hear about a particular topic, you might want to rethink your motive. They will probably be hearing what was taught but through children who have an imperfect understanding and interpret things through their own eyes. If you don't like a particular topic, you can consider teaching it at home. However, keeping them home and not teaching them is not a solution to your initial concern!

Puberty includes social, emotional, spiritual, intellectual, and physical growth. Growth happens in all areas, although the growth may not happen in all areas at once. It is easy to focus on the physical changes because that is what we can see and what your children can see. However, when teaching your children about puberty, it is important to consider the growth they will experience in *all* areas.

Socially, your children's friends are becoming more important. They want to blend in with their friends. They are worried about fitting in and may become more self-conscious. Their friends are now more important than you. Many parents struggle with letting go of children and allowing friends to take a front seat. A good way to let go of your children is to talk about friends a lot. Ask them what they think makes a good friend. Why do they like certain friends? How should you treat people that aren't friends? How do they feel when other people make fun of them or their friends? How do they feel when their friends are making fun of other people? Why is it hard to be a friend to someone? Teach your children how to choose good friends. Then you can let go because you know they are selecting children whose values are similar to theirs.

Emotionally, your children are dealing with conflicting feelings. They may be feeling excited and nervous about puberty. They may feel like they want to conform to their friends but be independent from you. They may feel more insecure. They have mood swings and crushes. Enjoy the moments when your children are having an emotional upswing. When they are down, ask what you can do to support them. If your children want privacy, give it to them. They may just want you to stop asking them questions for a day. Respect that they need time to evaluate what is happening to them and around them. This is a time where they are learning to sort their thoughts and evaluate their behavior and other peer behavior. This is a time when children start to spend some time alone. They may just want to think or listen to music.

Intellectually, children are now able to think more logically and abstractly (see Crain, *Theories of Development*). Children can understand abstract concepts, such as friendship. A young child would tell you the name of a friend if you asked them, "What is friendship?" Children in late childhood can describe the concept of friendship and give examples of good friendship behavior. This is a good time to begin or continue to discuss abstract concepts associated with sexuality, such as love, compassion, future, and freedom (choices).

In addition, your children are now spiritually under the influence of Satan. Feeling the Spirit is an abstract concept. Young children can feel the Spirit and respond to it, but it is not something concrete. Now that your children are beginning to understand the Spirit intellectually, it may be a good idea to have them be responsible for teaching a family home evening lesson on feeling the Holy Ghost. Find moments you can feel the Spirit and encourage your children to describe how they feel. When you are in a situation where you feel uncomfortable, talk with your children about how you feel and why you might feel that way. Ask them how they feel in this type of situation. Talk with your children about what you can do to find good feelings again. Feeling the Spirit will be essential for them in choosing correct sexual behavior (hugging, holding hands) as they move into adolescence and start dating.

Physically, boys' and girls' bodies are beginning the process of preparing for adulthood. They will be able to create a pregnancy or become pregnant. This is only possible after puberty occurs. Boys will experience physical changes, including testicle growth, pubic hair growth, early voice change, penis enlargement, ejaculation or nocturnal emission (wet dreams), growth spurt, underarm hair, later major voice change, and facial hair growth. Girls will experience physical changes, including breast budding, pubic hair growth, growth spurt, menstruation, and underarm hair. There is a variety of helpful books devoted to explaining the physical changes of puberty. They include illustrations, explanations, and glossaries. I have listed a few in the resource section. I suggest you refer to one of these more detailed books when discussing physical changes with your children. You can even include your children in choosing the book they might find most helpful in describing pubertal growth.

There are a few special issues to consider when discussing physical changes with your son. It appears that boys who develop late have a more emotionally difficult time adjusting to the physical changes of puberty (see Haffner, *A Parent's Guide to Raising Sexually Healthy Children*). If your son is developing late, reassure him that every child will develop when the time is right for him. However, listen to his concerns. Puberty is a big deal; just think back to when you were going through the experience. If you developed late, let him know how you felt. Boys can begin developing anywhere from ages 9 to 14. It then takes three to four years for the process to be complete. Boys may also be concerned about penis size. Again, listen to his concerns. Let him know the size of a normal penis, 2–4 inches when soft and 5–7 inches when erect. If he wants to measure his penis, let him. For boys that are concerned, this may assure them that they are normal.

Two other concerns for boys are erections and nocturnal emissions (wet dreams). As boys experience pubertal growth, erections become more common. They happen frequently and not always because a boy is sexually excited. Teach your son how to manage or cover an erection during a time when it might be embarrassing, such as in front of a class or walking down a crowded hallway. You can encourage him to cover himself with a book or fold his hands in front of his genital area until it subsides. Let him know that it's normal for his penis to suddenly change size. This is part of his body changing.

The first nocturnal emission is similar to the onset of menstruation in girls. This is not under a boy's control. As testosterone increases in a boy's body, there is a build-up of semen in the seminal vesicles (see Packer, "To Young Men Only"). When the vesicles are full, a signal is sent to the central nervous system signifying that it is time for them to empty. The emptying often happens during sleep, which is a nocturnal emission (wet dream). This will usually occur more than once for boys who are not sexually active or masturbating because whenever the vesicles are full, they need to empty. Consequently, the only outlet for emptying is through a nocturnal emission. Assure your son that you understand this is not under his control and he need not feel ashamed. You may let him start changing his own sheets if he feels more comfortable with this. Let him know this is normal and expected, so he need not fear something is wrong with him.

There are a few special issues to consider when discussing physical changes with your daughter. It appears that girls who develop early have a more emotionally difficult time adjusting to the physical changes of puberty (see Haffner, *A Parent's Guide to Raising Sexually Healthy Children*). If your daughter is developing early, reassure her that every child will develop when the time is right for her. However, listen to her concerns. Again, puberty is a big deal. If you developed early, let your daughter know how you felt. Girls generally begin developing anywhere from age 9 to 16. It then takes three to four years for the process to be complete. Girls may be concerned about breast size. If they are developing early, they may be worried that they are showing breasts while their friends are not. If they are developing late, they may worry that they have no breasts.

Breast development is probably the slowest pubertal change. Breasts are generally the first thing to start growing and the last to be complete (see Richardson and Schuster, *Everything You Never Wanted Your Kids to Know about Sex*). Breasts continue to develop until about the age of 17. Reassure your daughter and listen to her fears about breast size. Our society puts forth the model of small waists and big breasts to which girls are comparing their budding body. Reassure your daughter that her breasts will continue to grow more. At the same time, help her find things about her body she does like. Encourage her to focus on the parts of her body that she can control. If she has beautiful hair, compliment her on it and let her decide her haircut. If she has acne, help her find some cream or ways to manage outbreaks. Her self-confidence will grow if she can have parts of her body that she feels good about. Let her know that no gadgets, creams, or exercises can increase bust size. If you find your daughter stuffing her bra, be careful not to mock or ridicule her efforts. Gently ask her how she feels. How does she feel about her breast size? How does she feel when she compares with her friends? Do any of her friends stuff their bras? What does stuffing her bra accomplish? Gently let her know that stuffing her bra is only going to make her feel good for a moment. Ask her what she thinks she can do to feel better about her body. How can you help?

It is important to gently remind your children that outward appearance is not the most important thing. But remember that their bodies are changing of their own accord and this is difficult. There should be a balance. For every reminder you give that appearance is not everything, you should also be finding ways to help your children feel good about their own bodies. This is not sending a mixed message. Heavenly Father has given us a temple. Are temples beautiful places? Are the grounds well kept? Is the inside filled with beautiful paintings and furnishings? Yes. The inside and outside are both beautiful. Allowing your children to modestly follow clothing and hairstyle trends helps them feel like their outsides are beautiful, which contributes to happy, beautiful insides. Encourage them to follow the Word of Wisdom. This will help them feel energetic and healthy. Working on Personal Progress for girls or Duty to God for boys and other talents and gifts allows your children to feel beautiful on the inside, which will also help them feel their outward beauty as a daughter or son of God.

Young women and men have a tendency to sometimes feel jealous of one another's bodies. There is always someone with prettier hair, better skin tone, straighter teeth, longer fingers, a more ideal figure, and so forth. There is a tendency for youth to compare their bodies with someone else's and feel jealous of a feature that their bodies do not exhibit. There is a wonderful teaching moment in this jealousy because youth understand what it is like to want something someone else possesses. The one thing that Satan is jealous of is our bodies (see *Doctrine and Covenants Institute Student Manual*; D&C 93:35). He is so jealous that his main goal is to tempt us to destroy our own sacred bodies. You can ask your youth, "What things make you feel jealousy?"; "What does it feel like to be jealous?"; "What do you do when you are jealous?"; "What other emotions do you feel when you are jealous?"; and "How do you treat someone when you feel jealous of them?" You can explain that, even though their bodies are imperfect, Satan is incredibly jealous of them. Is there a part of their bodies Satan does not desire? No. He would take a crippled body with rotten teeth and scraggly hair! This is how important a body is. You can encourage your youth, when they are discouraged by their own bodies, to remember that even if they have bad acne, Satan would take their bodies if he could (and he is trying!). This is not always going to comfort youth who are experiencing the ups and downs of puberty, but they may gain an understanding of how important their bodies are and that they need to treat them with respect and honor. They will learn to value their bodies as a great gift from God.

The next topic with girls is menstruation. About two years after breasts begin to develop, the onset of menstruation will occur (see Haffner, *A Parent's Guide to Raising Sexually Healthy Children*). A mother or another trusted female caregiver can describe her own experience with her period. You can share when it started, how it felt, how you dealt with it, and how you felt about the timing. Take your daughter to the store and ask her what she thinks she might want to try as a sanitary napkin. You can share what you use and why. Let her choose a discreet place for them in the house. Show her how to use one. You can also show her how they absorb water. Then show her how to dispose of them. Explain that she should change them often to avoid infections. Tell her how you know it is time to change yours. Let her know that she might have a whitish discharge in her underwear sometimes. It is normal to have that discharge. It is a way for her body to naturally clean out unwanted bacteria in her vaginal area. If it is cheesy or smells bad, she should let you know. She might feel fresher and cleaner if she showers more often during menstruation. Give her sanitary napkins to put in her bag or locker and keep one in the car. Menstruation can start anywhere.

Personal hygiene can become an issue at any time during puberty. Because of increased activity in the sweat glands, body odor will need to be managed. Give your children deodorant and let them choose the scent and type. Allow them to try out different kinds to discover what they prefer. As soon as you notice an increase in body odor, allow your children to manage it with deodorant or through other means. If they say they are not ready for it, you can just let them know where it is so they can get it when they want it. Most will choose to use it.

Shaving will also begin during puberty. It is difficult for some parents to allow their children to shave because it means your children are growing up. However, if your children request to begin shaving, teach them the proper way to shave to avoid nicks and cuts. You may allow your children to try different ways of shaving to find out what is right for their needs. For example, my husband needs an electric razor to shave his face but a hand razor to shave his neck. Some children may be sensitive to certain razors or shaving creams or may feel more comfortable with an electric razor or hand razor. Allow them to try different methods to discover what will meet their needs.

If you don't teach your children when they want you to, a less experienced friend may teach them where you can't watch to make sure it is done safely. If your children haven't asked you about shaving by around age 12, you may want to teach them the proper way to do it. Then when your children are ready, they will know how to safely shave. Some parents want their children to wait until their first period or a particular age to start shaving. Keep in mind that your children will give you clues as to when they are ready. When they start to feel self-conscious about leg, underarm, or facial hair, it may be time to allow them to control these parts of pubertal development. It is up to you if you decide on an age or time period that seems appropriate for shaving. However, keep in mind that pubertal development is personal and children develop when their bodies are ready.

In school, boys and girls are taught the mechanics of pubertal development. Remember, you are teaching your children values associated with pubertal development. For boys, let your son know that his body is getting ready for being able to be part of creating children. For girls, let your daughter know that this means her body is getting ready for being able to have children. This is part of God's plan for men and women. Being able to help create or bear children is a sacred role, and your son or daughter is getting ready to be part of it.

Puberty is a time with intense and fluctuating sexual drives for youth. You can remind your children that sexual drive is part of the sacred process of pubertal development, and puberty is getting their bodies ready for sex. Also teach the value of sex in marriage. Part of the reason sex is reserved for marriage is because children are so important to Heavenly Father. Their spirits need bodies to experience this earthly life. They need a father and mother to raise them and should be conceived within marriage. The other reason sex is reserved for marriage is because it is the ultimate expression of love, passion, and commitment. It is a special way for a married couple to express their love and commitment to each other. Young teenagers have not developed enough maturity to understand adult love, passion, and commitment. Although their bodies are getting ready for sexual experiences, the time to actually engage in sexual experiences will be when they have entered into marriage.

Discussions on masturbation may need to be revisited. As children experience pubertal growth and their sexual organs mature, masturbation may become a common occurrence among your children's friends or peers. Masturbation is not only a male activity. Boys and girls will need discussions on masturbation. Church leaders have taught that around puberty, children should be taught about masturbation because teenagers may develop a "strong sexual appetite" through masturbation ("Talking with Your Children," para. 8). Your children may not have displayed any problems with self-exploration or masturbation in their development. However, they will still need to be taught about masturbation—what it is and why it is inappropriate.

Boys and girls should also know some basic information about the changes in the opposite sex. Remind them to be empathetic toward the opposite sex because they are changing and growing too. Boys should know that girls will be growing breasts, getting pubic and underarm hair, growing taller, and starting periods. I have a friend whose husband grew up with sisters. She assumed he knew all about menstruation. After she accepted his marriage proposal, she was surprised to learn that he knew nothing about periods or menstruation. She couldn't believe he had no idea what her body did every month to prepare for a child. How did he think babies grew in the womb? Girls should know that boys will experience testicle growth, pubic and underarm hair growth, facial hair growth, voice changes, growth spurts, and nocturnal emissions.

Most children will be hearing about the changes in the opposite sex at school, though not always formally. Children will talk. It is better for them to hear it from you so you can answer their questions and give them correct information. Also, opposite-sex parents should talk with their opposite-sex child. This is paving the way for knowing how to communicate with the opposite-sex partner in a relationship. Fathers *and* mothers should still hug and show physical affection for their sons *and* daughters. It is polite and respectful to ask for a hug during puberty if it seems appropriate. However, even if they say no, ask again another time. Their emotional state is fluctuating, and saying no one time does not mean they never want a hug again.

Sharing information about how you felt during puberty may help your children feel more at ease. You can share what concerns you had about your body. Share your concerns about your body, your talents, your feelings toward your parents, and other appropriate feelings. Express how you felt about the opposite sex. You can also share how you dealt with your concerns and feelings. This is not only good for your children but will also be good for you to remember the awkwardness, embarrassment, and emotions from this time in your life. It will remind you how important it is to be empathetic about your children's concerns so they may feel they can trust you to help them during this time.

Avoid teasing your children. You may think something is funny, but they are so tenderhearted and aware of the changes they are experiencing. Think back to how awkward and embarrassing things were for you. I remember my best friend's dad coming home from work one day to a brand-new training bra on the counter. This was his oldest daughter approaching puberty. My friend and I were very embarrassed when he asked, "Why do they call these things training bras? It doesn't train your chest to do anything." He sure thought he was funny, but we were mortified. Teasing may also contribute to your children avoiding asking you questions. They may already feel shy about asking you questions, so when you tease them you are essentially closing the door for communication.

A good way to provide children with correct information when they are feeling too shy to ask you is to give them a list of approved websites they can refer to for answers to questions. Sometimes they might not want to ask you, and that is okay. You can also buy them a book about puberty they can refer to on their own for answers. There are some websites and books in the resource section you can review, or you may find others. Give your children some freedom about where to go for answers to questions. This means you give them appropriate choices through approved websites and books. Make sure you still let them know that you are always available to answer a question if they want to ask. By giving them multiple resources for answers, you are keeping communication lines open. They may feel they can trust you more if you give them some freedom in finding answers they need.

15

Ages 9-11: Questions, Answers, and Ideas

"Our greatest danger in life is in permitting the urgent things to crowd out the important."

—Charles E. Hummel

Question and Answer

Q: What are hormones?

A: Hormones are special chemicals in the body that tell the body to change in some way.

V: All people have hormones. Boys and girls will both be going through hormonal changes during puberty and you should be sensitive to changes in members of the opposite sex.

Q: What is a normal-sized penis?

A: When it is soft, it is about 2–4 inches. When it is erect, it is about 5–7 inches.

V: Boys seem to be concerned about how big or small their penis is. You might hear boys or girls saying that sex is better with a bigger penis. Actually, most penises are about the same size when they are erect. It doesn't make any difference during sex how big or small your penis might be.

Q: What is semen?

A: Semen is fluid containing sperm that is ejected during sexual intercourse.

Q: What is a wet dream or nocturnal emission?

A: A wet dream is when semen is discharged from the penis while a boy is asleep.

V: It is normal to have wet dreams. It is your body's way of emptying your seminal vesicles because the vesicles can only hold a little fluid. When the vesicles are full, they need a way to empty.

Q: What is ejaculation?

A: This is when semen comes out through the urethra, where you urinate.

Q: How often do boys have erections?

A: They can have several throughout a day.

V: It can be embarrassing, but it is normal. It can happen even if you are not excited about anything. Your body is just changing.

Q: What age is normal to get your period?

A: Most girls have their period at ages 11 through 13.

V: Every girl will develop when her body is ready. It might be difficult when you have a period and your friends don't, or they have their periods and you don't. Some girls don't have their periods until they are 16 or 17, and that is still normal.

Q: What does a period feel like?

A: Sometimes you don't feel it at all. Sometimes it can feel like a little dripping.

Q: Does menstruation last until death?

A: No, it usually only lasts until you are 45–55 years old. Your body then stops making the hormone that tells your body to have a period. When your body stops having periods, it is called menopause.

Q: How long does a period last?

A: It usually lasts three to seven days.

V: Girls are all different, and their periods last for different lengths.

Q: What is regular?

A: Cycles are usually twenty-eight days, but it is common for young girls just starting to menstruate to not be consistent in the number of days before the start of the next period. Every woman is different and the timing of cycles will be different. Generally as you get older, you will get more regular, but some women never do have regular cycles. For those women, this is normal.

Q: How much blood do you lose during a period?

A: You usually lose about three to six tablespoons of fluid. It's also normal to have a few small clots. If you have big clots, let me know.

Q: Is it better to use tampons or pads?

A: You can use whatever feels most comfortable for you. Generally, a lot of girls start with pads. Tampons can be difficult for some girls to put in because the vagina is small and not used to having something inserted in it. Also, when using tampons, use great care to change them regularly to avoid infection.

V: Whether you use tampons or pads doesn't matter. Every girl can use what feels most comfortable for her.

Q: Can anyone tell I'm on my period?

A: No one can tell just by looking at you.

Q: What is PMS?

A: PMS stands for premenstrual syndrome. Hormonal changes that create a menstrual cycle can also create other symptoms like cramps, mood swings, bloating, back aches, breast tenderness, and a few other symptoms.

V: It is impolite to make fun of or ridicule girls who are menstruating or to assume they are menstruating because they are having a bad day. Menstruation is a wonderful opportunity for women because this process will eventually be part of creating a child.

Q: What is an elective abortion?

A: An abortion is when someone chooses to have a medical procedure performed to stop a pregnancy from progressing.

V: Some people choose to have abortions, but we believe that a baby is sacred. It has a right to life since it was conceived. If there is a situation where the baby will not be cared for properly by a married father and mother, we believe adoption will provide the baby with better opportunities in life.

Q: How do "accidents" happen?

A: Sex is pleasurable for adults, even if it doesn't sound like much fun to you right now. It is such a strong desire that some people have a hard time saying no to sex. An accident is when two people have sex and don't intend to get pregnant but do.

V: Sex is for marriage. If an "accident" happens in marriage, there are two people already in place to take care of the child. As you grow older, sexual desires can be strong. You will need to learn how to control your desire so it can wait for the appropriate time.

Q: What is a miscarriage (spontaneous abortion)?

A: A miscarriage is when conception has occurred (or a sperm and egg met and the egg implanted in the uterus), but for some reason the growing embryo or fetus didn't continue growing. The uterus then expelled (pushed out) the embryo or fetus.

V: Miscarriages can create many different emotions. A woman and man may feel sad, angry, upset, or relieved or may feel other emotions.

Q: What is AIDS and HIV?

A: HIV is a virus that causes AIDS. AIDS is a blood disease.

V: You can be friends with people who have AIDS, but you need to be careful when *any* friends have blood coming from anywhere on their body. You should find an adult to help you and not touch any blood. (If your children has been exposed to needles, been around a family member or friend who has used drugs, explain that they should never touch a needle but find an adult that can dispose of it properly.)

Q: What is oral sex? (You can ask your children first what kinds of sex people talk about in school or what they have heard before discussing this topic. If they have not heard about this kind of sex, you may ponder how you feel about teaching it to your child. Keep in mind that oral sex is common and they will hear about it. You should be the one to tell them the facts; decide whether you feel it is right to bring it up now or when they are 12–14.)

A: Oral sex is sexually stimulating the genitals using the mouth.

V: The value about oral sex will be a personal one. You should indicate that it is sexual conduct and should wait until marriage, if it happens at all. Let your children know they are normal if they do not engage in oral sex. Some people like it, and some people do not like it. Let your children know that it will be a personal choice for them and their partner once they are married.

Q: What is anal sex? (You can ask your children first what kinds of sex people talk about in school or what they have heard before discussing this topic. If they have not heard about this kind of sex, you may ponder how you feel about teaching it to your children. This kind of sex is probably not as common as oral sex.)

A: It is inserting objects, usually the penis, into the anus.

V: Anal sex is called sodomy. We believe that anal sex is not an appropriate form of sexual expression.

Q: What is an orgasm?

A: It is a powerful feeling you get from having sex. It is the part of sex that is the strongest pleasurable feeling. It is also called *climax*.

Q: What is a sexually transmitted infection (STI) or sexually transmitted disease (STD)? (There is a distinction between the two, but it is probably not necessary to explain the difference at this age.)

A: It is an infection caused by bacteria, a virus, or a parasite during sexual contact. This sexual contact can be oral, anal, or vaginal.

Q: Why is modesty so important?

A: Part of modesty is clothing yourself to protect and keep sacred parts of your body that are special. Part of modesty is also helping others keep their thoughts clean and pure.

V: Dressing immodestly is showing disrespect for those around you. I had a youth activity where a leader came in with a large fake piece of mucus hanging out of his nose. He gave a little talk about something fairly insignificant. Then he asked the youth why they kept staring at him. They pointed out the mucus. He then discussed how dressing immodestly distracts those around you and those you are dating from the true meanings of respect, friendship, and relationships. People around you become so focused on a part of the body that they lose focus on the vital components of any relationship. This is also a shallow piece of any relationship. Physical attraction is only a small part of a long-lasting relationship.

V: Dressing modestly can be coded many different ways. An easy guideline to remember is a head, shoulders, knees, and toes analogy. If youth can lift their arms up in the air over their head and show stomach, a shirt is too short. If they touch their shoulders and feel skin, they need sleeves or longer sleeves. If they can feel skin when they touch their knees, their skirt or shorts are too short. If they touch their toes and their skirt or shorts come up too far above the knee in back, they are too short. Help your youth find ways to modify current styles to also fit modesty needs.

Q: What is pornography?

A: Pornography is essentially *anything* that is intending to stimulate sexual arousal (*Webster's New World Dictionary,* 501). This can be pictures, movies, books, the way someone dresses, a particular gaze or way of looking at someone else, and so forth.

V: Pornography is detrimental to spiritual health and relationships. We believe pornography is something that should be avoided. If you ever come across pornography, it is best to walk away and let a parent know that you saw something. They can help you find ways to deal with the images or thoughts that are consequences of seeing pornography.

V: Part of the reason we teach modesty is to help you *not* be walking pornography. When you try on an outfit and want to buy it because it makes a part of your body sexually appealing, you are intending to sexually arouse someone. You become walking pornography in that outfit. This is different from an outfit making you feel attractive. When you wear clothes that draw attention to body parts, even if they are not the most sacred parts (like a back or stomach), you are walking pornography. The intent of those types of clothing is to draw attention to the body in a sexual way, to arouse someone.

Ideas for Conversation Starters

- Read books about sexual expression. Read books that include the mechanics of sexual intercourse and books that include the importance of love in the relationship.
- Read books about pubertal development (include both sexes for your children). Give your child books to read on their own and ask what they are learning, what they like, what they understand, what they don't like, and how they feel.
- Ask or read books about where babies come from, how a baby grows, why people have sex, sexual expression, who should have sex, different family forms, and anything else you have already taught them. Remember, they need to hear things more than once, just like you.
- Ask your children what the family believes about a sexual topic. Ask them why you believe that way.
- Ask your children, "Are there kids at school that like to touch kids in a way they don't like? Have other kids touched you in ways you don't like? What did you do? If not, how do you think you would handle it if they did touch you in a way you didn't like?"
- Ask your children, "Do you think boys and girls are treated differently? If yes, how? How does that make you feel?"
- Regarding friends or friendships, ask your children:
  - » What makes a good friend? How do good and bad friends treat you?
  - » How do you decide who you want close to you?

- » How have you helped a friend? How has a friend helped you?
- » What do you like to do that your friends do? What do you not like to do that your friends do?
- » How can you tell who is a true friend?
- » Can friends be different sexes or ages or come from different cultures?
- » Some people have lots of friends who aren't very close, some people have lots of close friends, and some people have a few close friends and lots of friends who aren't close; what do you like to have? What can you talk about with your close friends that you can't talk about with your not-so-close friends?
- » How do you make a new friend?
- » What are the benefits of friendship? The costs?
- » What do you do when one person wants to be a friend and the other person is not interested?
- » What makes you a good friend?
- » Do you think (a character on a media show or in a book) is a good friend? Why or why not? If the character is not a good friend, do they have friends? (They usually do.) Why do you think those people are friends with her (him) if she (he) is not a good friend?

- When do you think boys and girls should start dating? Do the boys and girls at your school date? How do you feel about dating? Why should you wait until you are 16 to start dating?
- Have you ever seen anything that made you uncomfortable (like pornography), but you looked at it because you were curious? How did you feel? How did you respond? How can you respond in the future? If you haven't seen these kinds of things, how do you think you would respond if you did? What can you do if a friend wants to show you inappropriate pictures? How would you feel?

Phase 3
Conduct Learners
(Ages 12+ and Premarital)

16

Ages 12+: Controlling Conduct

"Most powerful is he who has himself in his own power."

—Author Unknown

Children mostly learn facts and values throughout the beginning of their sexual development. They may also have learned some of the behavior that will be expected of them in the future. However, the teenage years are the most salient for shaping sexual behavior. Teenagers have the knowledge, the values, and the sexual development to now begin controlling their conduct. *For the Strength of Youth* is a great resource for giving your children guiding principles about correct conduct. Many of the topics relate to sexuality, such as friends, dress and appearance, entertainment and the media, music and dancing, language, dating, and sexual purity.

This chapter will add a few ideas to consider when talking with your teenagers about dating, kissing, necking and petting, and masturbation. Keep in mind that you will want to discuss these issues *before* your children are at the age when these things may start to happen. Ideally, you want to discuss these with your children at ages 12–14. There may be times your children pretend not to listen.

However, your children are listening, even if they don't appear to be listening. I was reading a book to my 5-year-old son one day when his 2-year-old little sister repeated a few sentences I had just read. She had been sitting across the room, playing with some toys. She did not seem to be paying any attention and wasn't interested in the subject of the book. But she had been listening!

In addition, teenagers respond more readily to question-and-answer sessions than lectures. You can start some of these discussions by asking them how they feel about dating, boys or girls, hugging, kissing, modesty, and other topics. You can also ask what they have been hearing at school or with their friends about these topics. Listen to their responses and try to understand how they feel. If you don't understand, ask why they feel the way they do. Give information as it comes up in the conversation rather than lecturing your children. The more open you are to listening to your teenagers, the more likely your children will listen to you and try to understand your point of view.

Dating

I dated a young man in high school a number of times. One particular date, he exclaimed, "You're not the kind of girl I date. You're the kind of girl I bring home to my mom and ask to marry!" I was quite confused at this comment and asked, "Don't you marry a girl you date?" He responded, "Yes, but I'm not getting married yet!" I'm not sure how he expected to find a wife later in life without first dating her.

For the Strength of Youth is clear to state that youth should wait to date until age 16, and even then they should avoid repeatedly going on dates with the same person (24–25). Because dating is preparation for finding a marriage partner in our society, it is better to wait to *steady* date until youth are closer to the age that they will begin considering finding a spouse. Sexual attraction and feelings are strong, especially as youth are just beginning to experience them and learning how to control them. Steady dating invites more opportunities for youth to engage in behaviors they are just learning to control! They need to develop the maturity and self-control to wait. Youth have sexual desires. These desires are good and natural, like hunger.

However, there is a time for them to mature and learn some self-control before they begin steady dating in preparation for marriage.

In *For the Strength of Youth*, youth are counseled to "avoid going on frequent dates with the same person" (25). What does *frequent* mean to you and your children? This is something you may decide or discuss with your children. This could be something you can bring up in personal interviews with your children *before* they begin dating. What limits will you set? Can they only date the same person once a month or after they have gone on a date or two with another person? Even if you set limits and need to adjust them as your children actually begin dating, it is important for your children to see the limits, know why they are there, and have some input as to what the limits entail. This will give them a sense of ownership, responsibility, and respect for the limits.

What is a date? This is a good question to discuss with your teens. Hanging out has become a common practice to replace dating. How do "hanging out" and "dating" differ? Elder Dallin H. Oaks gives a few good ideas for defining a date. The first idea is that it involves a commitment. There are two people who agree to spend time together for a certain time, in a certain place, and with a certain goal. This date may include other people, but the agreement is that these particular two are together within the group. Elder Oaks continues his definition with a "test of three *p*'s" he learned from his granddaughter: a date must be "(1) planned ahead, (2) paid for, and (3) paired off" ("Dating versus Hanging Out," para. 10).

Asking a young woman on a date can be an intimidating experience for a young man. As your teenagers begin to approach dating, remind them that *every* child is a child of God. Even if they do not want to go on a date with a particular person, they should *always* treat the other person with honesty, respect, and kindness. There are polite ways to decline a date without crushing the other person's feelings of self-worth. Discuss with your young woman how to politely decline or accept dates. Discuss with your young man how to politely ask for dates and politely accept a refusal. Dating does not need to be expensive or overly elaborate and creative. It may be appropriate for you to share some of your dating experiences, such as times you were rejected for a date, what you did for dates, how you approached saying good night, and other dating stories that may be of help for your children.

Kissing

The world has skewed the meaning and intent of kissing. When I was in college, a young man I was interested in often came over on weekend evenings. He would call up to me on my balcony if my light was on and ask if I wanted to hang out. We would usually watch a movie and talk. One night after watching a movie, we discussed kissing. He made a move to kiss me, and I rejected the kiss by moving away. He expressed a desire to kiss me to see if we had a "spark," because he only wanted to date girls with whom he felt a "spark." I had been quite attracted to and interested in this young man. He was kind and attractive. I had also seen a spiritual side of him at church that was appealing. However, kissing was not a determining factor in whom I should date. In fact, I was surprised when he wanted to kiss me because we had not even been out on one date. Though he came over to watch a movie occasionally, he had never formally asked me to accompany him anywhere as a date. In fact, he often would come over after he had just been out on a date with another young woman. We were still just getting to know each other. I told him I didn't kiss just anyone. And though I liked him, it was not enough for him to earn a kiss yet. My kisses were reserved for a committed relationship.

The world equates physical affection and attraction with love. A story in the news demonstrates the general devaluation of kissing. Neal McDonough, an actor, refused to film sex scenes on a television sitcom, "Scoundrels" (see Thompson, "Former Desperate Housewives Star Neal McDonough 'Fired from TV Series'"). He lost his job for refusing to do kissing and sex scenes. His reasons for not filming these kinds of scenes were his religious views and "his reputation as a family man" (para. 3). Many individuals have applauded his determination. However, when I saw online reviews and heard a local news station in Kansas City, Kansas, asking for people's opinions of Neal McDonough's actions, an overwhelming number of reviews and callers echoed the sentiment that Neal McDonough was "stupid." They believed that he was throwing away millions of dollars for just a meaningless kiss. "It's not like he was really cheating on his wife" was the idea. It was, after all, just a pseudo kiss on television to them.

The evidence of the devaluation of kissing is also seen in many relationships where the individuals feel they need to experiment physically with kissing and sex to see if they are compatible. One of the reasons couples decide to cohabitate is to determine whether they are well matched in all areas, which includes sexually (see Popenoe and Whitehead, "Should We Live Together?"). However, sex is an act of love. Therefore, love comes first. Love is not dependent upon a physical action but is supported and shown through physical action. Kissing is also an act of love, which should come after the feelings of love are present and not to determine whether love, or like, may be forthcoming in the future. Relationships that are created because a couple felt well matched physically are based on shallow motives and don't last long. When a better kisser or a more exciting partner is discovered, a relationship based on physical affection quickly crumbles.

Someone is usually hurt by a casual kiss. When I was in high school and college, I often heard the idea that you could be "friends with benefits." This meant that a boy and girl who were friends could kiss with no strings attached. It was just for satisfying a physical desire and there was no pressure for a long-term commitment. Unfortunately, there were no strings attached, at least for one partner. Too often, strings became attached for one of the friends because they would have liked to have been in a longer-term commitment. This partner would then often have feelings of guilt, shame, anger, hurt, jealousy, and sorrow. There really is no such thing as a casual kiss, for a kiss always means something. In the scriptures, one kiss was also the ultimate betrayal. Judas Iscariot told the chief priests and scribes, "Whomsoever I shall kiss, that same is he" (Mark 14:44). He betrayed our Lord and Savior with one kiss. Kisses can really hurt those relationships we should be protecting most.

Even Latter-day Saints with good intentions and desires make the mistake of falling for the world's view of kissing. It is saturating the lives of children through all means of communication. Kissing has become a recreational pursuit, not a demonstration of love. Youth see that sex is a black area (totally inappropriate). They are taught that sex waits for marriage. However, kissing can be in the white area (totally appropriate). The difficult part of kissing is that it is mostly a gray area (in between appropriate and not appropriate). Some appropriate kissing is suitable in the right relationship at the proper time. However, many youth and young adults are unsure when it is appropriate to kiss, whom it is appropriate to kiss, and what type of kissing is appropriate. Because there is so much gray area, Satan has a terrific set-up for leading youth down an inappropriate path so slowly that the youth do not understand what is happening until they are too close to or beyond the black area.

The good news is that youth want to do what is right! And now you know what to teach them! My husband served in the Young Men presidency in a ward with some wonderful youth. He set up a fireside where the youth could write questions on a slip of paper and put them in a basket. The youth did this during the entire fireside so if a question arose based on another question, they could ask it anonymously. One youth leader read the questions while a panel answered the questions. The panel consisted of a bishop, bishop's counselor, and stake president. One of the questions read, "When do you know if it is okay to kiss, and who do you kiss?" These youth wanted to know because they wanted to make correct choices.

Counsel with your youth and consider the who, what, where, when, why, and how of kissing. Who are you kissing? What is an appropriate kiss, length, and type? Where can I kiss (location)? When should I kiss? Why am I desiring a kiss? How do I feel before, during, and after a kiss? The answers to these questions are not concrete but are a general guideline for your youth to practice feeling and following the Spirit within certain parameters. Some youth begin kissing earlier than others. It is important to discuss kissing *before* your youth is actually participating in kissing. They are more likely to listen, create rules, and make decisions about kissing before it is time to kiss.

We encourage young children to decide *now* not to drink, smoke, do drugs, or have premarital sex. Why do we encourage children to decide about these things now? Well, we know that every action is preceded by a thought, whether the thought is followed up by planned action or spontaneous action. An action has to work through the brain as a thought before we can move any muscle because our muscles are controlled by the brain and our thoughts. When youth decide now what they will do (or not do) and how far they will go, they have already programmed their thoughts to be followed by particular actions. The action may be to stop, walk away, or suggest another activity. Whatever action is taken is a product of the programming or lack of programming a youth has in their brain and thoughts. This is also why we should encourage youth to decide *now* who, what, where, when, why, and how they will kiss. Kissing discussions will probably be most effective between the ages of 12 and 14. Youth at these ages are probably not kissing yet and still listen to you (most of the time). They are also not quite interested in kissing yet, which will help them make clear decisions that will become the basis of their future actions. Again, the ages I suggest are general, and you may feel your children may need a discussion at an earlier age.

Who?

Who are you kissing? Who should you kiss? Think back to my experience with a nice young man in college who wanted to kiss to see if we had a "spark." Who would I have been kissing? This was a nice Latter-day Saint young man with good standards. However, I did not even know his full name, his parent's names, or his siblings' names (or how many he had). I did not know his hopes or dreams. We were not exclusively dating. It was painful to reject a kiss from this boy because I really did like him and wanted to get to know him better. But I knew I didn't know enough about him to kiss him.

A good guideline for who to kiss examines not only what you know about the person but also, and more important, how you feel about that person. Because kissing should be a display of true affection, people you kiss should be limited to those for whom you care deeply. Teach your youth that there are many ways to show affection and attention. Encourage them to spend more time showing affection through other means, such as holding hands, writing notes, or performing a needed service for that person. As two people grow in their affection in a relationship, kissing may gradually become an appropriate means of displaying affection. Keep in mind that youth are counseled in *For the Strength of Youth* to avoid steady dating.

The time it takes to develop a relationship with true affection often involves steady dating. When steady dating can begin is a personal decision, preferably after high school or a mission. Keep in mind that this does not mean any kissing in high school is inappropriate. I am giving some ideas for potential guidelines.

Another consideration when determining who to kiss involves honesty (see Bytheway, "What Do Kisses Mean?"). I dated a young man in college for over a year. For me, the relationship was growing into something serious. Then one day he confessed he had been kissing another young woman. I felt deeply hurt and betrayed. The relationship immediately ended. It is important to be honest with yourself and those whom you are kissing. Kissing signifies a level of commitment in a relationship between a young man and woman. When you show this type of affection, make sure your heart is consistent with your actions.

When youth consider their knowledge and feelings for a special person, they can determine the honesty of a kiss. They will have a better understanding of who they might want to kiss. The bottom line is to "save your kisses" for those you are committed to and care about deeply (Bytheway, "Who Do You Kiss?" para. 14–16).

What?

What is an appropriate kiss, length and type? *For the Strength of Youth* counsels dating teenagers to avoid "passionate kissing" (27). What is passionate kissing? Passionate kissing is intense, "sensual" kissing (*Webster's New World Dictionary*, 471). The intent behind this kind of kissing is to arouse feelings of sexual excitement. The meaning of a kiss seems to be one of the most important factors in deciding whether a kiss is appropriate or inappropriate. If the intent is to arouse sexual excitement, the kiss is inappropriate. If the intent is to satisfy a physical desire, the kiss is inappropriate. If the intent is a brief display of affection and love, the kiss may be appropriate. Many youth want to know if French kissing (sometimes called "making out") is crossing a line. French kissing involves an open mouth, which usually stimulates feelings of sexual arousal. It is usually an intense and prolonged kiss. This looks like the definition for passionate kissing.

Many teenagers want to know, "How far is too far?" This question is usually based on the assumption that you are talking about kissing. Kissing seems to be generally regarded as an appropriate premarital display of affection. Therefore, the assumption is that the questions is asking, "How much kissing is too much kissing?" Going "too far" or "too much kissing" is also in the intent of a kiss. When you begin to have feelings associated with sexual arousal, you have gone too far. Kissing is appropriate when it is a brief display of "affection" (Von Harrison, *Is Kissing Sinful?*, 9). You love someone and want to express affection, so you may give that person a kiss. The intention of the kiss should have nothing to do with what is happening with your sexual organs but with the spiritual and emotional connection you have with a person.

It is difficult to control your thoughts and feelings when kissing. Counsel your children to decide beforehand exactly how far they will go. Do you feel that your intent is righteous when you give a kiss on the cheek? Do you feel that your intent is righteous when you give a brief kiss on the mouth? Do you feel that your intent is righteous when you begin kissing longer or opening your mouth? Only you know the point at which your righteous intent turns to a desire for sexual excitement or a means of sexual arousal. The bottom line is to save your long, passionate kisses for after marriage.

Where?

Where can I kiss? This question can mean two things: where as in body parts (such as the cheek, mouth, forehead, or hand), or where as in a place for kissing. Even if your youth does not ask this question, it is a good idea to discuss appropriate or inappropriate places for kissing. For example, it is inappropriate for youth to kiss in an empty house, a car, or a room with a closed door. It would be more appropriate to kiss on a doorstep or in a family room where they can be easily interrupted to help them avoid temptation.

Encourage your youth to come up with some rules for kissing. Once they are kissing a significant other, kissing will probably happen more often. A few ideas for some rules could be to kiss only when both feet are on the floor, when someone else is in the house, or only before a particular time of night, like a curfew. There are many potential rules that your youth could have, but encourage them to pick two or three that they will remember. The bottom line is to save your kisses for a place where you will not be tempted to kiss for longer or more passionately than appropriate.

When?

When should I kiss? Readiness for kissing includes not only an individual's readiness but also readiness in the relationship. Kissing usually invites a desire for more kissing. Once a couple begins kissing, it often becomes one of their central activities (see Bennion, "Questions and Answers: How Much Kissing Is Too Much?"). The efforts to learn about a significant other's personality, interests, likes, dislikes, dreams, wishes, spirituality, values, goals, and other important information may become trumped by the time spent kissing.

It is difficult to gauge an individual's readiness for kissing. It is usually partially dependent upon the person with whom the individual is dating. Counsel your youth to listen to the way they feel. If they feel uncomfortable at all with a kiss, it is better to wait. Counsel them to wait until they can comfortably talk about kissing with their significant other. Can you comfortably discuss kissing? Have you spent significant time as a couple getting to know one another?

Kissing does change relationships. Once kissing begins in a relationship, counsel your youth to set goals that encourage the couple to continue learning about one another. Keep in mind that you will not always know when your youth has started kissing. Discussions and counsel about kissing should come *before* your youth is dating. A sample goal may be kissing after spending significant time in another activity where there is time for continued learning about one another (not watching a movie). Some youth or individuals may feel that this is difficult because they want kissing to be spontaneous. Some may even feel that kissing loses some of its meaning if it has to be scheduled in this way. However, how often are necking, petting, and premarital sex scheduled? Usually, going too far is not scheduled. That's why it's important to schedule kissing! There can still be some spontaneity, but by setting limits around kissing, youth are avoiding a much more difficult problem.

If the meaning of a kiss loses its value because there are limits surrounding it, a reassessment of the relationship might be necessary. Enforcing limits doesn't mean you love a person less. In fact, you love the person more for the efforts that are required to practice self-control. This means the person loves you enough to respect you and avoid hurting you. The bottom line is to save your kisses until you feel ready and the relationship has sufficient substance. Then make an effort to continue learning about the person you are kissing.

Why?

Why am I desiring a kiss? I attended a homecoming dance my junior year of high school with a friend. We went with a group of good friends, none of whom were seriously dating one another. We had a lot of fun at the dance and during the other activities that were planned. At the end of the night, my date dropped me off at my house and walked me to my door. I thanked him and went inside. Later I found out that he was upset he had spent so much money on the date and didn't even get a kiss. He felt that I owed him one. What is your motivation for wanting a kiss? Is it social pressure, curiosity, attraction, pride, physical pleasure, lust, or love?

Kissing is a beautiful and essential part of a healthy relationship. Kissing is part of showing love. It is to be used as something good in a relationship, not misused as a vehicle for obtaining immoral desires. The bottom line is to save your kisses for times when you are motivated by love, not lust or other immoral desires.

How?

How do I feel before, during, and after a kiss? The who, what, where, when, and why questions all touch on feelings. Your children are preparing for the adult world and learning to be guided by the Spirit in all things. Most spiritual things are felt, not heard or seen. Counsel with your youth and help them learn to listen to their feelings. Are they uncomfortable with kissing someone? They should also consider the answers to all the other questions. Are they ready? Is it the right person? Do they have established limits or rules? What are their desires?

Another way to approach helping your children gauge whether the Spirit is guiding them or if they are just excited to obtain a kiss is to refer to the temple. A temple is a sacred, holy place, like your children's bodies and the bodies of the individuals they are kissing or dating. In guiding your youth to determine appropriate kissing, you may have them consider how comfortable they would feel kissing a particular person that way in the temple. Does it feel right and sacred? The bottom line is to *save their kisses* for when all things *feel* right in their heart.

NECKING AND PETTING

Kissing is usually the starting point for physical affection. If kissing is not appropriately limited to the right person, time, place, and desire, necking and petting may follow. *Necking* is defined as "intimate contact" and "passionate kissing" (Kimball, "President Kimball Speaks Out on Morality," para. 29). Passionate kissing has been described in the kissing section. What is intimate contact? *Intimate* is defined as "most private or personal" or "very close or familiar" (*Webster's New World Dictionary*, 341). *Contact* implies touching. Therefore, necking is intimate contact that includes private touching. This touching could consist of things like back massages, inappropriate dancing, kissing the neck or shoulder, or any other touch that elicits a sexual response and is not involving the private parts of the body.

Sometimes an innocent, nonsexual touch can elicit sexual excitement. Pubertal development is unpredictable and the swing of hormones and emotions may lead to times where innocent touches produce a sexual excitement. Encourage your youth to recognize sexual arousal or excitement. This is an essential part of relationships. It is not bad for them to experience sexual excitement. Their youth is just not the time to add fuel to the fire. Discuss with your youth what to do during a time when they feel sexually aroused, because it may happen at times where they are not doing anything inappropriate. You can give them scenarios and ask them how they might handle it. For example, your son is "hanging out" with some friends. A girl he is interested in comes over and places her hand on his arm to get his attention and talk to him. This excites him sexually. What can he do? This is an innocent touch. Counsel your youth to find ways to think about something else, change the topic of conversation, or change their physical position. In this scenario, he could change positions. If he is sitting, he can stand up and ask if she wants to go for a walk. He could ask if she wants something to drink. There are multiple ways for youth to manage their sexual arousal.

Petting is defined as "fondling of the private parts of the body for the purpose of sexual arousal" (*Aaronic Priesthood Manual 2*, 94). This, in turn, often leads to fornication, or sexual relations before marriage. Generally necking, petting, and fornication are not the first expressions of affection. Holding hands, kissing, and other similar expressions of affection are initially used to show you care about someone in a special way. Holding hands and kissing are not inappropriate, but they are the beginning of expressions of affection. If youth do not decide how far they will go and where they will stop, expressions of affection may continue to progress to necking, petting, and fornication.

I'll use an example to illustrate. When playing a video game, the goal is to complete every level. First, you play and reach a certain point in a particular level or complete one level. The next time you play, you might get to that same point more quickly. You might even go beyond that point, even if it's just a step or two. The next time you play, you move even more quickly through the familiar parts of the game. Then you get even farther on that level or progress to the next level. Every time you play, you make progress and go a bit farther. This is similar to what happens when youth engage in any expression of affection. Once you hold hands, it is easier to hold hands the next time. Once you kiss, it is easier to kiss the next time. The youth may then also begin to go a bit beyond where they have been before and kiss for longer or more often. Once you have treaded territory in expressing affection, you move through that territory more quickly and go a bit farther into the unknown territory. Often the place youth leave off expressing affection one night might be the beginning point for the next time they see each other. Youth may forget their goal, the temple, as they progress through different levels of affection. Youth need to set limits so they know when to stop "playing the game" and wait for the right time to reach the ultimate level in temple marriage. They need to know how to draw a line and practice self-control.

People often refer to "putting on the brakes" when finding the appropriate time to stop showing physical affection. I am going to use a cliff to illustrate where youth should put on the brakes. There is usually a gray area in showing physical affection. Kissing usually comes before the gray area because some kissing may be appropriate. Necking, petting, and fornication are off the cliff because they are inappropriate. Satan has a wonderful grasp on kissing because there is so much gray area. I believe kissing is his greatest tool in leading youth slowly off the cliff because it can be appropriate at times. This is why it is so important for youth to decide now where, when, who, what, why, and how they will kiss. They should know where to put on the brakes and stay far away from the edge of the cliff.

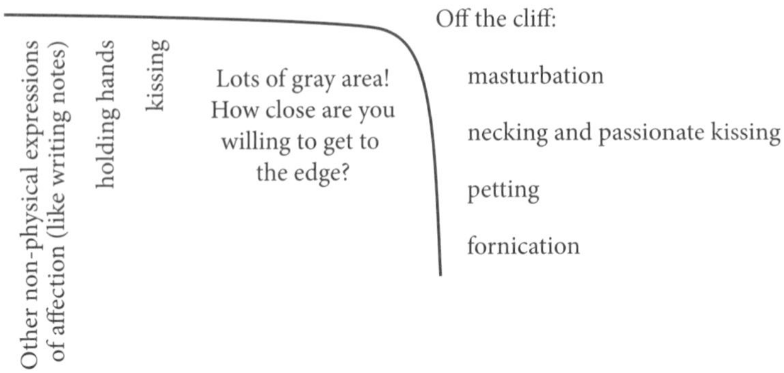

The other reason I like the cliff illustration is because it also illustrates the process of repentance. It is difficult to climb up a cliff once you have fallen off or climbed down. Often you can't do it alone. You need aids, such as ropes and another person to help you climb back up. When youth make mistakes and fall over the cliff, this illustration helps them understand that there is always a way back up. Jesus Christ's Atonement contains the aid and healing they need to repent and climb back up to safety. The illustration also shows that the farther you go in committing sin, the longer and harder the climb. It is much easier to climb back up when you are closer to the top. It is easier to stop and climb back up when repentance is required due to necking rather than petting or fornication. Masturbation is not necessarily "ranked" like necking, petting, and fornication. I just put it first because it is not ranked.

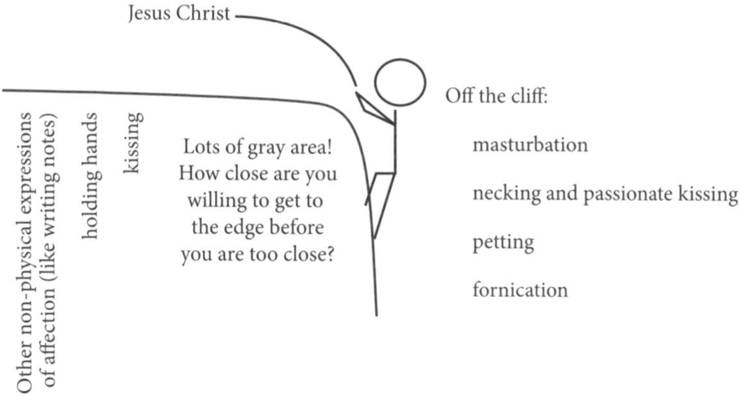

It is wise to teach your children about the "cliff" or another kind of line *before* they begin dating. And again, help your youth decide where they want to put on the brakes *before* they start expressing physical affection. Priesthood interviews with youth or a personal date with Mom or Dad are great times to discuss kissing, necking, petting, fornication, and other sexuality topics. Teach them about repentance during these discussions. It is easier and more effective to teach them repentance before they actually make mistakes. Then when a mistake is made, they may remember the things you have taught them. Alma and Enos are two examples of men who repented because they remembered the things their fathers had taught them (Alma 36:17; Enos 1:2–3).

Masturbation

The world has considered masturbation to be a normal and healthy part of boyhood in past years. Recently it has taken on new meaning. Masturbation is usually done alone, with no contact with another person. Thus there are no diseases that can be contracted from masturbation. Also, pregnancy cannot occur from masturbation. These two fear factors are usually associated with sex. The world is now claiming that masturbation is not only healthy but also a good alternative to sex (see Levkoff, "She-Bop & He-Bop"). It is becoming the new abstinence. This is what your children will be facing when they hear about masturbation.

We believe that masturbation is a sin (see *A Parent's Guide*). It can also create a greater desire for sexual experiences, which can be difficult to control. A young man's body produces semen continuously. There comes a time when the glands are full and need to be emptied. The body has its own natural process of emptying the glands through nocturnal emissions. When a young man masturbates, he is emptying the glands before they are full and empty naturally on their own. His body then begins to increase the production of semen, creating a need for the glands to be emptied more often. This generates a desire for the young man to masturbate again (see Packer, "To Young Men Only").

Young women are also being encouraged to masturbate in the modern world. Encouragement is given because masturbation is a way for young women to not be dependent on men for pleasure (see Levkoff, "She-bop & He-bop"). However, sexual organs were created specifically for the purposes of showing love in marriage and creating children, which both require a woman *and* a man. The world wants women to think that they should have a rewarding career and independence from men to feel fulfillment in their lives. However, teach your daughters (and sons) to be truly independent, which means to be "free from the influence or control of others" (*Webster's New World Dictionary*, 329). Independence does not mean being alone and doing everything without others. It means you can work with and around others and *not* be influenced by their attitudes and actions. In this way, you are teaching your daughter (or son) to be in the world but not of the world.

Both sons and daughters need discussions about masturbation throughout their teen years. It is pervasive in our modern culture. It may be difficult for them to understand how it can harm them when there are no physical damages caused by masturbation. When discussing the consequences of masturbation, help them understand that the greatest negative effect of masturbation is the loss of the Spirit. If appropriate, share your own experiences with masturbation. This could be how you overcame or controlled the temptation or how you felt if you experimented with it. Keep in mind that you need inspiration when discussing topics like this, especially if you are sharing personal information.

So What Is Appropriate?

When talking about sexuality, a lot of our language uses *no, don't, stop*, and *abstinence.* This kind of negativity is not always easy for youth (or parents). Our youth may feel that we are building a huge brick wall around them, with every block engraved with *no, don't*, or *stop*. These words can feel suffocating. This is a time in your children's lives when they are fighting for some freedom. They are learning about independence, responsibility, and relationships. Parents may understand that rules and *no*'s are important for freedom and independence because the consequences are positive when guidelines are followed. Youth are beginning to understand this but may not have realized the full impact yet. They are still learning about consequences and how limits actually protect them.

Unfortunately, there seems to be a lot of advice surrounding sexuality that focuses on what *not* to do and what to avoid. There is very little on what *to* do. It is important to focus on the good and what youth can do. Our bodies are marvelous creations! But because there are a lot of *no*'s, explain to your youth the reason for this. We don't want to focus on what not to do. We want youth to know the great things in which they can be blessed to participate. However, we do not have things spelled out for us all the time because different actions are appropriate for different individuals. We want youth to have parameters in which they can participate in activities but also have freedom for personal decision. Youth and young adulthood are wonderful times when individuals are learning to better understand and follow guidance from the Spirit. Let your children know that you are giving them guidelines so they will be able to determine the best course of action by following the Spirit. You give them the distinct wrong and a guide for how to tell what's right. Then they are free to choose what parts of right they feel good about participating in.

In addition, teach your child the difference between what feels *good* and what feels *right*. Some things feel good for a moment, but guilt, remorse, or shame later become the prominent feeling. When something only feels good, there is usually a physical or worldly appetite that is being satisfied. For example, I'll refer back to the young man I knew in college who thought a kiss determined my likability. It would have felt good for me to kiss him in that moment. I liked him, and kissing feels good. However, doubts would have quickly replaced the feelings of the kiss. Since kissing determined whether he would have had a "spark" with me, I would have questioned whether he felt that spark. I would have worried and felt rejected if he went on a date with another young woman after our kiss. Also, I would have felt ashamed and regretted kissing him if he decided not to continue dating me. Just because it would have felt *good* didn't mean it would be *right*.

On the other hand, when something feels good *and* right, the Spirit is supporting a thought or action. Feelings of happiness and joy will follow decisions that are made when you feel the confirmation of the Spirit. For example, after I dated my husband for a few months, the relationship felt right. He was the right person and it was the right time. When we finally shared our first kiss, it felt good *and* right. It was a beautiful experience that was accompanied by feelings of joy, happiness, and confirmation by the Spirit.

It can be difficult to tell the difference between good and right. Your child will probably make mistakes in judgment when they try to distinguish the difference. These mistakes are still important for their learning. Be patient and try to share moments when you just feel good or when you feel the Spirit so you can help them learn to tell the difference. This process should begin when your children are young but takes on a new meaning when your children become youth engaged in learning about the opposite sex.

17

Ages 12+: Love and Relationships

"Lust is easy. Love is hard. Like is most important."

—Carl Reiner

The best way to teach children about love and relationships is to make sure they have examples of good, healthy relationships in their lives. I have a friend who dated her husband for six years before she finally decided she would marry him. It took her a long time to make a commitment because she had never seen a relationship work in her life. The bad examples had made her afraid that she would also not know how to foster a healthy relationship with her own spouse. We know the power of example is a salient factor in our children's lives. Let's look at what we can teach them beyond being good examples.

Crushes

Youth will have crushes. My first crush happened when I was 14 years old. I never spoke to the young man; I knew his name but nothing else about him. I had a crush on him for my entire eighth grade year. I was too scared to talk with him, but his name (and mine with his last name) decorated many of my course notebooks that year. It is common for youth to have crushes. They may or may not be friends with their crush. They may or may not end up dating their crush. Crushes prepare youth for understanding feelings of love because these are the first real feelings of attraction they experience.

It is easy for adults to see the futility of some crushes. However, for youth, these crushes and feelings are real. It is important for parents to acknowledge that crushes are normal and healthy. It might help to remember what your first crush felt like. You probably *do* understand what it's like to have a crush. Feelings are an important part of love. Try to validate your children's feelings. If your children's behavior, school work, or other responsibilities begin to suffer because they spend so much time daydreaming about their crush, then you can discuss the importance of feelings not getting in the way of responsibilities. Otherwise, crushes are important to youth and part of learning to love. It might be wise to ask them *why* they have a crush on a particular person. What is it about this person that is so worthy of their attention? These discussions may help them realize what qualities they like and don't like in another person. Or if they don't know why they like a particular person, asking this question may help them analyze what it is about this person that sets the butterflies in motion.

Love versus Lust

Lust and love are easily confused, especially for inexperienced youth. Passion, excitement, enjoyment, and need can all be incorrectly classified as love. I had a good friend in high school who was often "in love!" She had a new boyfriend every few months that she "couldn't dream of living without" because they were "so in love." I quickly realized a pattern in her relationships. As soon as the newness and excitement of the relationship wore off, she would begin complaining about the imperfections of her current boyfriend. Within a few weeks, they would break up, and she would have a new boyfriend.

The media plays an enormous role in perpetuating unreal love. Many romantic movies show the courting phase of a relationship, where everything is new and exhilarating. These types of movies generally end with a wedding, some other type of commitment phase in a relationship, or the illusion that there will be a commitment. We are only viewing the get-to-know-you fun. There is wonderful romantic music and no awkwardness in knowing when or how to kiss or hold hands. Things just happen naturally in perfect romantic rhythm. It's no wonder our youth are confused about real love. They are often shown only one phase of love, and this is the phase so easily confused with lust.

Lust and love are antonyms. By definition, *lust* is a "bodily appetite" and *love* is "strong affection" (*Webster's New World Dictionary*, 385, 383). In these simple definitions we can see the "natural man" and "saint" as described by King Benjamin (Mosiah 3:19). The natural man yields to bodily pleasures and appetites while the spiritual man (described as a saint) yields to God the Father. In teaching your youth about lust and love, you can help them determine the difference by looking to their desires. Do they like someone because they are popular or cute and dating them would look good to others? Do they like someone because they have seen them treat others with kindness and therefore feel affection for that person? This may be a good beginning for determining the difference between lust and love. Youth may still get confused, but this is a step in differentiating between lust and love.

Knowing when love is real can be difficult. Most youth realize that real love includes trust and honesty (see *Kiss and Tell: What Teens Say about Love, Trust, and Other Relationship Stuff*). Ask your youth why they can trust particular people or how they know they can trust someone. You can also ask them how trust and honesty impact a relationship. You can also help your youth understand that real love includes compromise, respect, and effective communication. Let them know things you have done with your spouse to solve problems (or have another trusted couple discuss this with them if you are a single parent or their other parent is unavailable). Ask your youth what it means to respect someone and how to show respect. Priesthood interviews with a father or father figure (or mother interviews) may be a good time for parents to ask youth questions about love. They can ask for their children's perspectives on how they might know they are in love, what it takes to nurture love, and what love may include. This interview could give you an idea of what topics you might need to address with them.

You can share your feelings from the beginning of your courtship with a loved one and how those feelings have grown and changed over time. Let them know how you have nurtured your feelings. There are generally two ways we nurture feelings of love. One way is to use words to express how we feel. These words can be written or verbalized. For example, my husband likes to receive notes describing what I love about him. Another way to show love is through actions. Cooking, cleaning, dating, and other actions show love. It's great to be an example and go on a date with your spouse, but you can also occasionally tell your youth why you date your spouse. Your children may not always know why you do the things you do. It's easy to take for granted that they understand why you go on dates or kiss one another good-bye. They may not always realize the reason, even if they see the love you are showing through example. One day I came home from grocery shopping and found a note in the fridge with a plate of lunch. My husband had explained to the children that I worked hard and he wanted to show his love and appreciation by getting my lunch for me so I wouldn't have to do it when I came home. His thoughtfulness showed me and the children, through actions, how he continued to nurture the love in our relationship.

Love is a chemical reaction. It begins with the chemicals in the brain that create feelings of pleasure, a wildly beating heart, and obsession (see "The Science of Love"). You feel good when you are around the subject of your affection, you get butterflies when you see that person, and you can't stop thinking about them. This is why youth have crushes. There is a chemical reaction in their brain. If the relationship is nurtured, it can develop into love.

Once the brain becomes accustomed to the higher levels of the first love chemicals, the pleasure, wildly beating heart, and obsession disappear. It's like being on drugs. You would more of the chemicals to keep the same reaction. This doesn't mean you've fallen out of love, though. Many people, like my high school friend, interpreted the disappearance of these feelings as falling out of love. However, after the brain has adapted to the first chemicals, a new chemical helps a couple retain feelings of love for the long term (see "The

Science of Love"). These chemicals are generally released after sexual experiences. Isn't it interesting that the chemicals releasing exciting feelings bond a couple during courtship? Then sexual experiences chemically bond a couple during marriage for the long term. This is more evidence of the importance of sexual experiences in marriage. But they can be harmful outside of marriage when love is just beginning.

Love is an important lesson in our lives. Learning to love is like learning how to share or do something else that requires effort. It takes practice to get it right. Youth need to have some time interacting with the opposite sex so they can practice how to recognize feelings of love and how to appropriately express love. They also learn the qualities they like and don't like in other people. You can be a guide for your youth in helping them understand which feelings of love are maturing and which are lustful. You can also guide them to know how to appropriately express their feelings of love.

A word of caution about youthful love: Youth have been counseled to wait until the age of 16 to date (see *For the Strength of Youth*). Even then, they are encouraged to group date until they are ready to look for a marital partner. Coming to love another person takes some individual, personal time together. Parents should use prayer and personal revelation in helping their youth determine what to do if feelings of real love are developing with another individual before they are ready for marriage. If your youth is group dating but continually seeing only one person while group dating and developing intense feelings for this person, you may need to review with your youth the *reasons* for the limits. They may be following the limits but not understanding the reasons for the limits. Again, use prayer and personal revelation to guide your youth during their dating years.

18

Ages 12+: Abstinence Only

"Train up a child in the way he should go: and when he is old, he will not depart from it."

—Proverbs 22:6

I had a fear of spiders growing up that didn't end until recently. The basement in my childhood home contained a few black widow spiders, which are venomous. Therefore, they are dangerous for children. My parents warned us not to go in a particular part of our basement where the black widows liked to hide. My siblings and I were fearful of being bitten by one of these infamous spiders. We used to turn the light on and run past that part of the basement if we needed to pass by it. My heart used to pound and I'd keep looking around to make sure there weren't any spiders near me. We also didn't know much about the spider and believed what anyone would tell us. I believed that the spider could jump eight feet to bite me (and would if I didn't run fast enough).

Last year as an adult, I was fearful of another infamous spider, the brown recluse. We were living in a basement with our two small children. Spiders were everywhere, and they were huge. I was terrified that one of the children would be bitten. I prayed continually that we would all be safe but continued to fear for our safety. I was having a hard time identifying the most common spider I was finding in the basement. I wasn't sure what was meant by the "violin" mark found on a brown recluse. I thought it was found in a place similar to the hourglass on the black widow spider. I finally did some research and found reputable Internet sites where I could learn about both of these spiders. After learning about the spiders, when they come out, what to do to prevent them from living in your home, and what to do if bitten, I calmed down. I didn't need to be as fearful as I had been. I took the precautionary measures recommended (like keeping clothes off the floor, putting spider traps under the beds, and so forth). I kept a copy of a medical guide about spider bites with our medicines. Then feeling empowered, I prayed to Heavenly Father and let Him know that I had done my part and the rest was up to Him to keep us safe. What happened after that would work itself out if I had faith.

There are many things that parents may be afraid of when considering sexuality and youth. Parents often fear that their children will engage in sex outside of marriage. They fear that if they teach about birth control, their youth will think it is okay to have sex. Some parents use fear as a motivator for teaching youth not to have sex. They instill a fear of diseases or pregnancy as a way to discourage sex outside of marriage. Parents can unintentionally use fear as a motivator for teaching youth to refrain from sex by emphasizing physical consequences. This can inadvertently create a fear of sex in youth rather than a fear of God and a healthy respect for their body and others' bodies.

Faith versus Fear

When we only fear the consequences of something (like being bitten by a spider or disease or pregnancy from premarital sex), we become consumed by the emotion of fear. It blinds us and can prevent us from making correct decisions or from thinking clearly. While I was fearful of the spiders, I was always watching for the spiders but would have panicked if I saw one. If a spider had bitten one of my family members, I would not have known what to do. Similarly, fear can blind youth who are making decisions about sexuality. Fear of what other people think of them, fear of the physical consequences of sex, and fear of losing relationships are a few fears that may plague youth. Fear prevents youth from feeling what is right and wrong through the Holy Ghost. Fear also does not teach youth what they *should* do. When youth have knowledge of sexual topics, they will know how to respond and what they can do when placed in situations that require a decision. Knowledge can replace fear and give youth faith to do what is right, just as I had faith only after I replaced my fear of spiders with knowledge.

The scriptures teach that fear does not come from God: "For God has not given us the spirit of fear; but of power, and of love, and of a sound mind" (2 Timothy 1:7). Fear is a tool from Satan to blind men. It creates a darkness that suffocates faith. Our youth need to have the spirit of power, the spirit of love, and the spirit of a sound mind regarding sexuality to combat the pressures of the world.

First, have we instilled in them the spirit of power? Jesus Christ taught, "If ye will have faith in me ye shall have power to do whatsoever thing is expedient in me" (Moroni 7:33). We teach our youth to have faith in the things they have been taught throughout their lives. Do they have faith that their body is a temple of God? Do they have faith that everyone is their spiritual brother or sister? Do they have faith that if they follow the commandments, God will grant them the Spirit to aid in decision making? Do they have faith that prayer will help them be not led into temptation (Matthew 6:13)? This faith will give them power to make correct sexual choices. They can have power to withstand temptation and control their sexual desires.

Next, have we instilled in them the spirit of love? Charity is the "pure love of Christ" (Moroni 7:47). Youth with a spirit of love see others as Christ sees them. These youth would not treat another person without respect and kindness. Therefore, these youth do not engage in inappropriate sexual conduct because they do not want to defile or hurt another person. They feel Christ's love for themselves and others. Has your child developed the pure love of Christ? Have you encouraged and helped your youth work toward completing the Duty to God or Personal Progress awards? Working toward these awards give youth a chance to personally gain a testimony and develop Christlike attributes. The spirit of love is important for withstanding sexual temptations by loving others enough to treat them with respect in words and actions.

Last, have you given your children the spirit of a sound mind? If we break these two words down into their respective definitions, we find a profound meaning when they are combined. *Sound* can mean "free from defect, damage, or decay," "based on valid reasoning," "thorough," or "honest, loyal" (*Webster's New World Dictionary*, 616). *Mind* can mean "memory," "opinion," "intellect," "reason," or "the seat of consciousness, in which feeling, thinking, etc. takes place" (411). Let's put a few of these meanings together in a sexual context and see the clarity we can find. *Sound mind* can mean:

- Intellectual knowledge about sexuality, free from defect or decay (free from worldliness). This means parents have taught children the facts of sexuality, along with the added spiritual components.
- Honest reasoning in deciding appropriate behavior with the opposite sex. This means youth make honest judgments about readiness for kissing and other aspects of a physical relationship. This means they are honest with themselves and others about feelings and behavior.
- A consciousness free from defect or decay. This means youth make wise choices, such as avoiding pornography, that lead to a consciousness free from worldly pollution.
- A thorough memory for gospel and secular knowledge about sexuality. This leads to the ability to make correct choices regarding sexuality because they have knowledge about behavior and consequences that can be recalled when necessary.

Many possible combinations of these definitions exist that can enlarge our understanding of a sound mind. The most important thing to remember is that the definitions include a need for previous knowledge of the spiritual and secular facts so that the mind can make correct choices when placed in a position for decision. When our youth are armed with proper sexual knowledge that we, as parents, have done our best to impart to our children, we can have faith that our youth will make correct decisions or repent when they make mistakes.

Fear and Birth Control

Another fear many parents have is about birth control. They think that if they teach their youth about birth control, they will be implying that it is okay to have sex. However, research indicates that knowledge of birth control does not encourage sexual behavior (see Collins, Alagiri, and Summers, *Abstinence Only vs. Comprehensive Sex Education*). There is no official policy on birth control in The Church of Jesus Christ of Latter-day Saints (see *Handbook 2: Administering the Church*). Since no official Church policy exists, it's difficult to know whether or not to teach it to youth. The general trend seems to leave it to couples who are getting married to learn about birth control. However, this trend leaves youth with myths and misconceptions about birth control. They may not understand the functions and purposes of birth control. They may not even know that there is no official Church policy on birth control or assume birth control is bad because no one will talk about it. My ideas here are guided by scriptural principles, but every parent should be using prayer and spiritual guidance as they decide what to teach their children.

Again, the Church has no official policy on birth control. This may mean that there is not an official policy on *using* birth control. This does not necessarily mean that children should not be taught about birth control. Joseph Smith said, "In knowledge there is power" (*Teachings of Presidents of the Church*, 265). This can be applied to birth control. Your children can make correct decisions about birth control when they *know* about it. They may not be making decisions about how to *use* it, but they will decide how they *feel* about it. Youth and young adults may have already heard about it from friends. Many believe it is used because someone is "sleeping around." However, many youth and young adults use birth control for medical reasons. It may be difficult for them to use, or they may feel the need to hide its use because the feelings associated with youth using birth control are generally negative.

Again, there is no official Church policy on birth control. However, many young adults getting married believe that Heavenly

Father doesn't support birth control, and therefore He will have them get pregnant only when He wants them to. I have had multiple friends who believed this and did not begin birth control when they were married (thinking they wouldn't get pregnant until Heavenly Father wanted them to). They were surprised to get pregnant so quickly! Many of them have told me that after the first surprise child, they believed in birth control. Heavenly Father has all power. There will be times when He will trump birth control, or there will be times when a couple struggles to get pregnant. However, the union of a male and female body was made to create life! If we don't prevent things sometimes, neither does Heavenly Father. We have our choices and with those choices come consequences.

Youth can be taught the reasons for using birth control. Planning a family, regulating menstruation, and medical issues are all possible reasons for using birth control. They will be hearing about birth control at school and other places. Keep in mind that what they are hearing might be incorrect or portraying birth control negatively. Parents probably do not need to go through each type of birth control and what it does to the body to prevent pregnancy. Birth control options change often. When it comes time for them to talk with their future spouse about birth control and choose an option, their medical doctor and spouse will be their best sources for deciding which birth control option to use, should they choose to use it at all.

Youth should be taught that there is no official Church policy on birth control. Counsel them that this will be a personal decision when they are getting married. My husband and I had different bishops when we were engaged to be married. When we met with each bishop before our marriage, we received counsel. One of our bishops counseled us to not wait to have children and to have as many as we could. The other bishop counseled us to wait to have children because our marital relationship was the most important relationship. We would need time to develop and strengthen our marriage before inserting another person into the family. My husband and I counseled together and came to a conclusion on what we felt was right for our relationship based on the advice we had been given. We did not believe that one bishop was uninspired. We believed we had been given our range of choices that we needed to consider before we got married.

Fearful Conclusion

Fear is an ineffective way to persuade youth to stay morally clean. It may appear effective, but the long-term consequences may reach further than anticipated. I have made mention of my Latter-day Saint friend who confided in me that she cried after intimacy for an entire month after marrying her spouse because she had been taught to fear being morally unclean. Her intimate times with her spouse were tainted with her fear of being morally unclean. She knew she was not transgressing any laws, but the fear had been so deeply ingrained in her that she was fighting the difference between her fear and her knowledge. How sad that something so beautiful and right was tainted by fear! Teach your youth to have faith that they are making right choices by staying morally clean. Teach them that Christ will provide ways for them to escape temptations if they will follow the commandments. Teach them that even if they make mistakes, they can repent and be guided to do what is right. Give your youth faith, not fear, to make correct choices.

19

Ages 12+: Questions, Answers, and Ideas

"Seek first to understand, then to be understood."

—Steven R. Covey

Question and Answer

Q: What is douching?

A: Douching is a word for washing out the vagina. Some people think you should douche to keep yourself fresh and clean. You do not need to douche unless a doctor tells you to, because it can cause irritation or infection. The vagina has its own way of naturally cleaning itself out. If there is an unpleasant smell, you need to see a doctor.

Q: What are the "bases"?

A: The "bases" are a way for people to describe how far they have gone physically with another person. There is no standard definition for what happens at each base. It seems to generally start with kissing at first base. A home run would be intercourse. Second and third bases are usually necking, petting, or oral or anal sex.

V: A lot of people talk about which base they have been to, but not everyone is honest or understands the bases because there is no standard definition. Because we believe sexual relations are so sacred to a marital relationship, we do not talk about sex and physical relationships in this way. It demeans the beauty of a physical union and the person you are sharing this experience with. When friends are discussing things like this, you can find a polite way to leave or change the subject.

Q: What is a vibrator?

A: This is an object that is used for self-pleasuring, generally for women.

V: Using a tool like this or similar objects is considered masturbation. (You may need to refer to the masturbation section as you answer this question. Use spiritual guidance for what your children may need).

Q: I like someone who doesn't know I like him. How can I tell him? How do I know if he likes me?

A: That's a tough question. It's difficult to know if someone likes you. It's also difficult to tell someone you like him.

A: Think back to what your first crush felt like. Ask your children more questions than giving answers. They may be able to find a way to invite their crush to activities or other places where they can become better acquainted. You may share how you felt during your first crush and what you did. Encourage them to find others with the same qualities they seem to like in their crush. This will help them not focus so much on one person.

Q: My friend is doing something he shouldn't be doing. How can I help him?

A: Ask your youth, "What do you think you can do? What have you tried already?" Continue to be that person's friend in ways that are possible. Invite him to places where you feel comfortable. Let him or her know you are willing to talk about anything. When you feel prompted to say or do something (or not say or do something), then say or do it (or don't do it).

V: We love people, even if we don't love what they do. Make sure you are not placing yourself in dangerous or unholy places. Try to be as supportive as you can, but avoid situations that make you uncomfortable.

Q: When am I ready to have sex?

A: The easy answer is "when you are married." It can be more complicated than that. You may be essentially cutting off a wonderful sexuality discussion with your children if they are looking for help and you close the discussion at marriage. They are probably looking for signs of readiness for sexuality. Remember, you are not going to be able to make your children's decisions. However, you can be influential in their understanding of readiness if you are open to discussing what it feels like to be ready for a sexual relationship. Your children may also be thinking of a friend or family member who thinks she is ready to engage in sexual behavior. They may be looking for advice they can give their friend or family member or validation over a concern for that person. There are many factors that are included in sexual readiness. A couple should have consent from both parties to engage in sexual activity. If either partner feels any pressure, they are not ready. The couple needs to be able to talk about contraception and disease protection and be able to obtain it. Mature love and intimacy should be present in the relationship (both parties being able to share feelings and details of their lives).

V: Sexual intercourse should wait until marriage. However, you are loved regardless of the choices you make. I will listen and talk when you need me. You can also encourage your child to visit reputable websites like *Sexuality and U* (http://sexualityandu.ca/). This may also be a useful resource for them if they are trying to find answers or help a friend or family member.

Q: What are "blue balls"?

A: This is a term for blood that is built up in the genital area (arousal) for females or males and is uncomfortable because an orgasm has not released the build-up. You may feel cramp-like pain or tenderness. It is not serious and will not cause complications. The discomfort will go away with a reduction in arousal.

V: Some people may use this as an excuse to try to pressure someone into having sex (oral, vaginal, or anal). Some people may recommend masturbation to alleviate the discomfort (see masturbation section for information and values on masturbation). It is not serious and will resolve itself on its own, even if it is uncomfortable for a while.

Q: How far is too far? (Again, this answer is based on the assumption that you are talking about kissing with your child. Therefore, the assumption is that the question is asking, how much kissing is too much kissing?)

A: Too far is when you begin to have feelings associated with sexual arousal. Kissing is appropriate when it is a brief display of "true affection." You love someone and want to show it, so you give that person a kiss.

V: It is difficult to control your thoughts and feelings when kissing. You might want to decide beforehand exactly how far you will go. Do you feel that your intent is righteous when you give a kiss on the cheek? Do you feel that your intent is righteous when you give a brief kiss on the mouth? Do you feel that your intent is righteous when you give a long kiss on the mouth? Do you feel that your intent is righteous when you begin rubbing your partner's back or opening your mouth while kissing? Decide where you might feel that your righteous intent turns to sexual excitement.

Q: What is birth control?

A: There are different ways of preventing the sperm and egg from meeting so a pregnancy is less likely to occur. This is called birth control.

V: The Church of Jesus Christ of Latter-day Saints has no official policy on birth control. This is to be a personal decision between you and your future husband or wife.

Ideas for Conversation Starters

- Ask your youth, "What are you learning about in your sex education or health class right now? How do you feel in the class? What do you feel about what you are learning? How do other kids in the class seem to feel?"
- Ask your youth, "What would you do if someone started to pressure you to have sex? What do you think someone might say to pressure you to have sex? What are the benefits and costs of having sex?"
- Ask your youth, "How far do you think you might want to go with someone? What do you think your friends are doing? How do you feel about what your friends are doing?"
- Ask your youth, "Some kids at your age start to date; how do you feel about dating? Have any of your friends started dating or going out? What would you say if your friends ask why you aren't dating yet?"
- If you see many advertisements with young, pretty, slim models or handsome, strong models, you can ask, "Why do you think those models seem appealing? How do they make you feel? Do you know many people that look like that? How do you think that person feels about themselves?"
- Ask your youth, "How do you feel when your friends dress immodestly? How easy or hard is it to find modest clothing?"

20

Premarital Advice

"It is the timing that is so vital. It is wrong to do even the right things at the wrong time in the wrong place under the wrong circumstances"

—Spencer W. Kimball

Last summer, a daughter of one of my friends got married. This young woman had been a virgin, and my friend wanted to discuss some things about sex and marriage with her before her wedding night. She was troubled when she tried to bring up the discussion of sex in marriage because her daughter immediately told her she didn't want to discuss it with her mom. I asked my friend how she had talked about sex with her daughter while she was growing up. She said she hadn't talked with her daughter about it because she thought it was something you did right before marriage. Plus, it wasn't something happening in her daughter's life until this moment. She decided that with her younger children, she should probably discuss sex with them now so when the time comes for marriage they will feel comfortable talking with her.

I hope this book is encouraging you to begin talking with your children about sex at appropriate times throughout their lives. When it is time for your children to marry, they should already know the facts about sexuality, the rules of behavior and how to control themselves, and the spiritual reasons and benefits of sex and chastity. By the wedding most, if not all, of your *instruction* about sexuality should be completed. You have been reinforcing values throughout your children's youth and will continue to reinforce values throughout your children's life.

When your children reach engagement, there are a few things you might advise them to do while they prepare for marriage. Your advice should include a few words on rules and behavior, preparing for the marriage, and medical preparation. You may feel inspired to share other topics with your children as you pray and ask for heavenly guidance.

RULES AND BEHAVIOR

President Kimball shared a story where two young people committed sexual sins in their relationship (see Kimball, "President Kimball Speaks Out on Morality"). They told him that they had been justifying their actions because they "belonged to one another." Satan can easily find justifications for an already engaged couple to bend rules. A couple spends a lot of time together when they are engaged, which opens more opportunities for sexual indiscretions. Also, an engaged couple is now promised to one another, therefore inviting justification of any physical sexual actions that wouldn't have been committed with someone who was "just dating."

Rules of conduct, or limits, continue to be the same as when your children were "just dating." *Marriage* is when the rules of conduct change. Counsel your engaged young adults to continue exercising control. Remind them that the rules of conduct remain unchanged. It might also be wise to suggest the newly engaged couple create "rules" that may help them avoid sexual indiscretions. Some rules may include keeping four feet on the floor when kissing (no sitting or laying down when kissing, no kissing in the car), cuddling and kissing only when the door to the room or place you are in is open and other people are around, and setting a curfew (like midnight). These rules are things that a couple should have been doing when they were dating, but some couples tend to relax these rules when they are engaged. There is an endless supply of potential rules. Encourage your children to set a few rules (too many will be overwhelming) that maintain the integrity of the relationship. These rules should be sufficient to help the couple maintain their purity in preparation for marriage.

A friend of mine thought rules were a great idea and set some boundaries with her fiancé. Unfortunately, these simple rules were broken quickly into the engagement. As the engagement progressed for a few months, the simple broken rules became major sexual indiscretions. They were unable to be married in the temple. Rules are of no consequence unless they are heeded. Encourage your child that if they slip up on a rule, like breaking curfew one night, they should not justify or continue the action. They can reestablish the rules with their fiancé or decide whether the rules need adjusted to accommodate their particular needs.

Prepare for Marriage

I have a wonderful friend who was married in a courthouse by a justice of the peace. Her husband was in the military, and there were circumstances that prevented them from being able to plan a more formal wedding. My friend admitted to me that she was disappointed with this because she had always dreamed of a nice wedding.

Many couples focus on making their wedding day "perfect." They use all their energy and time planning the decorations, invitations, pictures, gowns, tuxes, timing, location, registry, and so forth. What seems to hide during the engagement is the fact that the wedding is only *one* day. It is a beautiful, marvelous day. But planning a wedding and planning a marriage are two different concepts. Again, planning a wedding is *one* day; planning a marriage is preparing for *eternity.*

With this in mind, encourage your children to find time with their fiancé to discuss expectations for their marriage. Because this book is focused on sexuality, encourage your children to pick a date and talk with their fiancé (probably close to the wedding date) about their sexual expectations. It might be wise to give them some reading to do with their fiancé so they can be prepared for the more intimate aspects of sexuality that are personal for each couple. My husband

and I read *The Act of Marriage* by Tim and Beverly LaHaye. We loved the book because it covered information relevant to a married couple that you didn't need to know before this time (sexual positions, how to stimulate orgasm). It is also written by a Christian couple who bases the information on the Bible. We did find some information that we may view differently as Latter-day Saints. However, the book was informational and helpful. We also read *What We Wish We'd Known When We Were Newlyweds* by John and Kimberly Bytheway. It gave some action steps that were helpful for us as we began our lives together. This book directed us to *The Act of Marriage.*

Many useful books and resources are available for engaged couples. You may have friends with recommendations for other books. Your children may even have recommendations from leaders. It is wise to encourage your children to select a few books to read with their fiancé. They are gathering information they will need to create a successful *marriage.* But they still need time to enjoy planning a *wedding.*

Medical Preparation

As part of discussing sexuality with their fiancé, your children will also need to do some medical preparation. Men and women should get a physical exam before marriage. Encourage your children to visit the doctor and discuss the medical decisions they are making with their fiancé. It is important for your children to be frank and open with the doctor. Women will be getting a pap smear, perhaps for the first time. Before a woman goes in for her premarital pap smear (or a man for his physical), she and her fiancé should have already discussed whether they would like to start a family right away or begin birth control. During a woman's doctor visit, she will discuss either birth control options or prenatal information based on her and her fiancé's decision.

If a couple decides they would like to begin birth control, the doctor can explain the options that would be best for this particular woman and her fiancé. Before going to the doctor, the engaged couple can research the different birth control options and have an idea of what they might like to try. The doctor may have more information after an examination that may direct a couple to try a particular method. Keep in mind that often birth control requires a period of time before it becomes effective in preventing pregnancy. If a woman schedules a doctor visit right before marriage, she may not have time for her birth control to begin its effectiveness until *after* the honeymoon. It is best to schedule a doctor visit soon after engagement. This leaves time for birth control to become effective. A woman can then have time to try a method of birth control and see if it works for her. Many women switch birth control because they dislike the first one they try due to side effects or inconvenience.

If a couple decides they would like to start a family right away, the couple should let their doctor know. The doctor can give advice and information about keeping the body healthy and about the normal time the couple should expect to get pregnant. A woman may be advised to do certain things, like take prenatal vitamins. She may also get information about what to do when she suspects or finds she is pregnant. Men may also be advised to do certain things, like avoid alcohol (which they should be doing anyway, of course).

Another medical issue facing some women is a small vaginal opening. As a teenager, I would randomly hear that sex hurts. I didn't understand this because sex was never portrayed in the media as painful. The hymen is a piece of tissue that is located at the opening of the vagina. When it is stretched during first intercourse (or through other things like inserting a tampon), it can cause pain. Bleeding can also occur when the hymen is stretched.

There is something women can do to help stretch the hymen before marriage to prepare it for sexual intercourse. Women can ask their doctor for a vaginal dilator. These are made in various diameters. A small dilator is used first, barely larger than the vaginal opening. This helps stretch the hymen with minor discomfort. Once the opening can easily accommodate the first dilator, another larger dilator is used to stretch the opening a little more. This process can take weeks. It is best for a woman to ask her doctor about vaginal dilators at her first premarital pap smear appointment, which should occur at the beginning of the engagement. This will allow plenty of time for stretching the hymen to a sufficient size so that intercourse should not be painful. There may still be some soreness and tenderness from exercising new muscles, though.

Engagement is an exciting time for a couple. These few points on rules and behavior, preparing for marriage, and medical preparation are things most couples will need to address during engagement. As you counsel and advise your children, you can help give them inspired information that will make their transition to marriage a little smoother.

SECTION 3

SPECIAL TOPICS

21

Homosexuality

"Never look down on anybody unless you're helping him up."

—Jesse Jackson

Homosexuality is increasingly becoming a part of our children's sexual world. It is regularly viewed on television, portrayed through social media, and has increasingly been a topic of political debate for same-sex rights. Children will be hearing about homosexuality and will likely know someone who is homosexual. As your children begin puberty, you will need to discuss homosexuality. An essential part of teaching children about homosexuality is portraying sensitivity in treating other temples with kindness and respect. Homosexuals have also been given a temple. It is not our responsibility to judge them. It is our Christlike obligation to be kind and respectful to them.

Often, when I ask men how they would feel if their son declared he was gay, they respond, "That would never happen, no way, no how!" These kinds of comments instill a fear and belief in children that they are not allowed to talk about homosexuality. It also displays a general feeling of unkindness or disrespect for homosexuals as a group. If children feel they can't talk with a parent about potential homosexual feelings because they know parents will treat them with the same attitude, to whom will they go for advice or answers?

When I discuss homosexuality in groups, I have a volunteer stand. I ask, "How would you respond if your child came to you and said, 'Mom (Dad), I think I'm gay'?" Responses are usually laced with disappointment, disgust, disbelief, unbelief, anger, sorrow, loss, fear of the unknown, and fear for the child's future and safety. I have the volunteers slide a piece of paper displaying their initial feelings under their foot. I have them slide another piece of paper under their other foot that says, "negative comments," denoting negative comments (jokes or other intolerant comments) parents or others may have made about homosexuals. Last, I have them put one hand palm down on a table and put a piece of paper under the palm labeled "lecture." This represents the response that many parents have to lecture their child about why homosexuality is wrong, not just the sin of sexual behavior. After they have covered these three pieces of paper, I ask them to walk across the room to a piece of paper labeled "Spirit." However, they are not allowed to uncover the three pieces of paper they are hiding with their hand and feet. I do this because these are feelings a child is hiding or combating and are not easily shared. It's incredibly difficult to move across a floor hiding three pieces of paper!

This demonstration illustrates how difficult (but important) it is for us to listen and lovingly respond to our children when they come to us with possible feelings of homosexuality. It also illustrates that we need to be kind in our language. If we are unkind in general to homosexuals as a group through our attitudes and comments, our children will feel the need to hide their feelings if they believe they may be homosexual. When they hide feelings, it is difficult for them to feel the Spirit. The Spirit will be essential in their lives in helping them cope with any confusion or challenges they may face with homosexual feelings.

One way to help our children know that they can talk with us about anything, even homosexual feelings, is to teach them to love sinners, not sins. Have you ever been tempted to steal, lie, cheat, or gossip? Have you ever been tempted to be angry or judgmental? We are all influenced by the "natural man" (Mosiah 3:19). These temptations do not necessarily make us sinners. When we actually steal, lie, cheat, or gossip, we have sinned and then become a sinner. Just because someone has homosexual feelings does not make them a sinner. If they engage in inappropriate sexual behavior, they are committing a sin. We do not encourage the sin, but we do love the sinner.

It is difficult at times for adults to separate their feelings and love the person, not the sin. For children, it is even more difficult. Children are cognitively immature. This makes it difficult for them to separate behavior from a person's innate goodness and divine worth, especially when most of the "good" and "bad" labeled for a child is related to behavior. If you tell children they did something bad, the children think *they* are bad. If you tell the children they did something good, they think *they* are good. Even adults sometimes have a hard time separating behavior from divine worth. When dealing with homosexuality, divine worth must be separated from behavior because homosexuals need an incredible amount of support and love to help them manage their behavior and successfully navigate through the storms in their lives.

Part of parents' concern with their youth being homosexual is the belief that there is a "degree" of sin greater than opposite-sex fornication. In *True to the Faith*, the heading "Homosexuality" refers you to "Chastity" (84). Homosexual activity is deemed a "serious sin," as well as fornication, adultery, and sexual abuse (30). There is not a degree of severity among homosexuality, fornication, adultery, and sexual abuse. They are all grave sins. It is the immorality that is the sin.

Often, another part of parents' concern with their youth being homosexual is the belief that the youth has already engaged in immoral behavior. We all have sexual desires during our pubertal development. That is the purpose of puberty, to sexually mature us for the opportunity to create a family. Sexual desires are a God-given opportunity for happiness, bonding, and pleasure in a marital relationship. Our youth are feeling these desires and learning to harness them. Just because a youth comes to you and says, "I think I'm gay," does not mean he is engaging in inappropriate sexual activity any more than a youth asking about birth control is engaging in fornication. We expect that our youth may have a sexual desire for a member of the opposite sex and be able to withstand that desire. Youth with sexual desires toward members of the same sex are also able to withstand that desire and stay morally clean. However, they are more likely to stay morally clean if they have your love and support in helping them manage their desires. As I have taught parents, it seems that the general attitude is that youth who declare they are homosexual must be sinning (engaging in inappropriate sexual relations). If you make invalid assumptions, you may close communication line that is essential for righteous support.

How do you respond if your children think they are homosexual?

First, homosexual feelings are generally not present until a youth is actually experiencing or has completed puberty (see Dank, "Coming Out in the Gay World"). Puberty is the maturation of sexual organs and is the time when a youth begins to actually experience sexual arousal. These organs may feel good to rub before puberty, but the sexual arousal and experience becomes mature at puberty. If your youth thinks they may be homosexual and have just begun puberty, ask questions such as, "Why do you think you are gay, lesbian, or homosexual?" and "What are you feeling?" If they are young youth, they may be concerned because they thought a member of the same sex was "cute." That does not necessarily make them homosexual. Youth hear friends talk about homosexuality and may believe that because one "symptom" is present in their life, they might be homosexual. Listen to your youth's questions and encourage them to continue living a chaste life. Encourage them to wait to make a decision whether they believe they are truly homosexual until they are sexually mature. Let them know you love them and will love them whether or not they are homosexual.

If your children have completed puberty and announce they are homosexual, respond with love. Ask what you might be able to do to encourage and help them in developing their talents, interests, and careers. Keep your arms open. If they decide to act on their desires, continue to treat them with love and respect. Your home may be the only place they feel the Spirit. Remind your children that the rules of the home will not change, but your love for them will also not change. The Spirit is the gateway to inspiration, and one day they may need to feel that Spirit. You can provide that through loving encouragement at home.

In addition, this may not be a "phase" that your children will outgrow. Trying to pray it away or talk your children out of it, even if done gently, will not make things change. By doing this, you are communicating that you don't believe them or love them for who they are. You can pray for strength, inspiration, and guidance for your children. We do not know much about the cause of homosexuality, but "individuals do not choose to have such attractions" (see "Love One Another: A Discussion on Same-Sex Attraction"). Homosexual *behavior* is a choice but feelings of homosexuality are not. Acknowledge your children's feelings and listen to them. Ask them how they feel. Ask how their choices will affect them. A friend of mine said that the day after her child announced his homosexuality, he appeared sad. She asked, "Don't you feel better? I thought that telling us would lighten your burden. If it didn't make you feel better, then why did you tell us?" She also reminded him that he was the same person he was before he told her and that she loved him just the same. That seemed to lift the weight off his shoulders instantly. This wonderful response allowed her to give support for her son, who needed to know he was still loved. Homosexuals do carry a heavy burden and need those around them to help make that burden lighter.

Your youth should already have been taught the plan of salvation, our purpose on earth, the importance of family, and the Atonement of Christ. If they are struggling with homosexuality, they may already feel guilt for not being able to conform with principles they know to be true. Parents should use prayer and revelation to help them best meet the needs of their homosexual children. Constantly reminding them of their nonconformance to the plan of salvation may lead to greater guilt, which drives away the Spirit. Find ways to help them better themselves and focus on positive activities that will uplift and strengthen them while they face this problem. The Church has provided an incredible new website, www.mormonsandgays.org, dedicated to encouraging, uplifting, and inspiring those who deal with same-sex attraction.

22

Homosexuality: Questions, Answers, and Ideas

"By swallowing evil words unsaid, no one has ever harmed his stomach."

—Winston Churchill

Question and Answer

Q: What is a homosexual, gay, or lesbian?

A: A homosexual is a person who loves another person that is of the same gender. A gay man is a man who loves another man, like your mom and dad love each other. Or it is a woman who loves another woman the way your mom and dad love each other. Women who are homosexual are sometimes called lesbians. This is different from the way you love your friend (insert name of same-sex friend). The way you love your friend is called friendship love. The way homosexual people love and the way your mom and dad love is called romantic love.

V: Heavenly Father has taught us that this special kind of love with sexual actions should be between a man and a woman. However, we should love all people, regardless of the way they feel about other people. We can't always help the way we feel about another person.

Q: How do I know if I'm gay?

A: That's a tough question. If your children have just hit puberty, they are usually too young sexually to determine sexual orientation. You may need to remind your children what it means to be homosexual. It means that a person is sexually attracted to members of the same sex. Like or love for a friend of the same sex is not the same thing as being sexually attracted to members of the same sex. Also, being curious about their own bodies and development and that of their same-sex peers is not the same as sexual attraction. Many youth are concerned about whether they are developing "normally" or how they compare with their same-sex peers. "Checking out" others of the same sex can sometimes be confused with attraction when it might be merely a comparison. To find if children are homosexual, ask if they have had sexual desires and know what it feels like. Are they sexually attracted to someone of the same sex?

V: We love all people, regardless of their sexual orientation. If your child is sexually attracted to people of the same sex, let them know you love them. Also, let them know that they can still choose their behavior. They still need to remain morally clean.

Q: How can I prevent my child from becoming homosexual?

A: Homosexual feelings are not a choice, just like sexual arousal from members of the opposite sex is not a choice. Our choices come from our behavior and thoughts based on those feelings. However, Satan is doing his best to confuse children and youth. Provide an environment in the home that invites the Spirit. Do the things our prophets have commanded us to do to strengthen our homes, like reading scriptures as a family and individually, holding meaningful family home evening, praying as a family and individually, and regularly attending meetings. In addition, you can do other good things that invite the Spirit, like holding callings and serving. You can also help your children learn what it means to be a good friend and how to choose good friends. These friends will strengthen them in their youth and help them make wise choices.

V: You can't necessarily prevent homosexuality, but you can prepare your family spiritually to make wise behavioral choices if you face homosexuality within your family.

23

Sexual Abuse, Harassment, and Rape

"Child abuse casts a shadow the length of a lifetime."

—Herbert Ward

Sexual abuse is devastating for those who become its victim. This topic is particularly close to my heart because my mother was a victim of sexual child abuse. She is still working to overcome the hurt, betrayal, and diminished self-image lingering from sexual abuse that began more than fifty years ago and lasted more than fifteen years.

Preventing Sexual Abuse

Parents want to protect their children from sexual child abuse. However, many parents don't know what to do to protect their children. They may take precautions, such as checking the national sex offender registry when moving to a new home or discussing inappropriate and appropriate touches with their children. However, what else do you do?

Children don't have much power over abuse by adults or children who are a lot older than them (see Richardson and Schuster, *Everything You Never Wanted Your Kids to Know about Sex*). We can teach children about respecting bodies and what areas of our bodies are only for certain people. However, some adults can still abuse them. Adults are bigger and stronger and have better reasoning skills. Also, most sexual abuse is committed by someone the child knows, likes, and is close to (see Kendall-Tackett and Simon, "Perpetrators and Their Acts"; Wattleton and Keiffer, *How to Talk with Your Child about Sexuality*). In fact, more than half of all abuse is committed by a father, stepfather, or father surrogate. It is more likely for your child to be abused by a family member or close friend than a registered sex offender living down the street. This means your child is probably around the perpetrator often because this person is regularly a part of your lives. This can make it difficult to prevent sexual abuse.

The best thing we can do for children is teach them that when or if someone touches them in *any* way that makes them uncomfortable (this doesn't have to be sexual), they should tell a trusted adult. Then *listen* when your children tell you they didn't like the way someone was touching them, even if it was just a dislike for tickling or pinching cheeks. This builds trust. Your children know you will listen if they tell you something bigger, like someone touching their genitals. Reporting abuse is an essential skill for young children because prevention is difficult. Children who tell an adult can then get help to address the feelings they are experiencing related to what happened to their body. They can get medical help more quickly. They can also be removed from the perpetrator more quickly, thus reducing the chances of repeat offenses.

Another consideration for preventing sexual child abuse is to spend time with your children. Play with them. Read to them. Go on outings with them. A convicted felon of child abuse once said, "I can walk into a playground and at a glance pick out the child who will go with me. It's the one who needs more time with an adult. Most adults don't see that" (see Wattleton and Keiffer, *How to Talk with Your Child about Sexuality*, 130). The more time you spend with your child, the less likely they will be to look for adult companionship with others who might harm them. Children crave adult attention and love. Make sure they get it from you.

In addition, children act out their world through play. If you take time to pretend play with your child, you may learn some new things they haven't articulated to you. For example, when our son started kindergarten and came home his first day, I asked what he did and what he liked. He told me a few things about his day. He was really excited and eager to talk about what he had experienced. However, when I was playing school with him later, I learned three times as much about what happened during his day than I did when he was just telling me about it. He was acting out things that were hard for him to articulate. When you play with your children, you can learn more about their lives and how they see the world, especially when they are in the role of the adult or other authority figure. It is also a setting more comfortable for them to show you what is happening.

What Do I Teach My Child?

There are a few specific things I advocate teaching young children. First, the best prevention any parent can invest in is the power of prayer and personal revelation. If your children want to go to a sleepover, birthday party, or other event and you feel uncomfortable, explain to your children how you feel and keep them home. Heavenly Father will keep your children safe if you do all you can do (2 Nephi 25:23). If something happens to your children and you have done all you can do, know that Heavenly Father will help you and your children. He sometimes allows things to happen because He does not take away our agency. But He then provides a way for comfort and healing through the Atonement of Jesus Christ (Alma 7:11–12). It is then our responsibility to continue trusting in Him and having faith in His Atonement.

Small children should be taught that anyone who tells you to lie to a trusted adult (mom, dad, grandma, grandpa) is not telling you something good. Make sure they know the difference between a good secret (a birthday present) and a harmful secret (someone hurt someone else and threatened them not to tell). Teach them that it's okay to tell on these people. Guide them with the Spirit. You can use feelings as a director for your small children. This is why we are given the Spirit, and it usually comes as a feeling! Encourage your children to express themselves when they are happy, sad, angry, scared, jealous, hungry, silly, and so on. Help them label how they feel regularly. You can teach your children that when someone makes them feel scared, fearful, or uncomfortable, the Spirit is telling them that they need to try to get away. If they can't get away, they should let you know as soon as they can. They can tell you how they felt and what happened. Also teach them to pray for help when they have these kinds of feelings.

We don't want children to fear other people in general. Sometimes, teaching children that there may be bad people out there trying to touch them in inappropriate ways may unduly instill fear in them. This is why I advocate teaching children that *any* touch that is disliked or uncomfortable should warrant the ability to voice their feelings and stop that type of touch. Then when they are uncomfortable if someone tries to touch their genitals, they are used to telling people to stop. Or they will let you know what has happened and know you will listen. The unfortunate thing is that many adults aren't willing to listen when children tell them to stop. I've seen this often with my son. He does not like being tickled, but the loving adults in his life tend to ignore his pleas to stop tickling. This is not malicious but a general attitude that he is just a child and that they, as the adult, know that he really likes to be tickled because it makes him laugh. However, just because it makes him laugh doesn't mean he likes it. Often I have to step in and gently remind them that he asked them to stop. Teach your children to listen to others by listening to them. Teach them that you will listen to them by actually listening!

Also avoid giving children the impression that only bad, sick, crazy, and mean people would hurt them. The book *Berenstain Bears Learn About Strangers* illustrates this principle (see Berenstain and Berenstain). In this book, Sister Bear is friendly and regularly talks to anyone. Brother Bear tells Mama and Papa Bear that Sister is always talking to strangers. Papa tells Sister that there are mean, bad, scary people in the world and that she should not talk to strangers. Sister is then scared of everyone she doesn't know and suspects them all of being bad, mean, or scary. Mama Bear sees Sister's distress and teaches her about strangers using an apple analogy. She explained to Sister that most apples are good and sweet. There are only a few that are bad. She pointed out that some apples look perfectly fine but are rotten inside, while others look different and are sweet and good inside. We need to be watchful for the bad apples, but we can still enjoy most apples, even ones that look different. This helped Sister realize that not everyone was bad, mean, or scary. She could still be friendly and say hello to people she met. She just needed to be cautious about accepting rides and other favors from adults she didn't know.

Most young children need explicit instructions on accepting favors from strangers. Again, because most abuse happens with someone the child knows well, be careful about not scaring them or teaching them to fear all strangers. I explain to my children that if a stranger asks for directions, offers to let them look at a puppy, or offers them candy or toys, they should not approach that person until they have found a trusted adult to go with them (mom, dad, grandparent, babysitter). I do not tell that the person may want to harm them. I explain that Mom and Dad like to know the people they are around, so they need to find us first before approaching someone they don't know.

Next, children also need to be taught appropriate names for body parts. We already discussed the importance of appropriately naming body parts. There is an added dimension to knowing body parts when considering sexual abuse. Children need to be able to accurately tell you what happened to them if they have been molested by an adult or child. I met a young child once who had been molested. She told her dad she was stabbed in the bum. Because this child didn't know the difference between her vulva or vaginal area and her buttocks, her dad couldn't figure out exactly what had happened to his child. If children need medical attention due to sexual abuse, it may be helpful for the children to be able to accurately describe what happened to them.

Something to consider when talking with your children about touching is that genital touching can feel good. This is part of the problem with labeling touches good or bad. There is appropriate touch and inappropriate touch. Even inappropriate touches can feel good. If we label touches as bad, children generally associate that with something they dislike or something that will hurt. Our genitals were made with the purpose of feeling good. Young boys may rub their penis and young girls may rub their vulva because it feels good. If an adult rubs a child in this area, physically it may feel good to the child. However, it will most likely make the child feel uncomfortable. Teach your children that these areas of the body are sacred and special. They are reserved for a special time in marriage. When this area is touched, it can feel good physically, even if they feel uncomfortable. However, these kinds of touches should wait for an appropriate time. The discomfort is the Spirit telling them they should try to get away or tell an adult if they can't get away.

Teaching relationship messages can also help children avoid sexual abuse or becoming an abuser. Relationship messages are communication about love, intimacy, and respect. These messages are often given by example in the way a spouse or child is treated. When we treat children with gentleness, kindness, and respect, they will learn how to use these qualities in their interactions with others. Relationship messages may also include discussions about love and trust. Explain to your children what love and trust mean and how your children can be loving and trusting. If children are learning how to show love in appropriate ways, how to show respect for all ages, sexes, and ethnicities, and how to communicate effectively with others, they are more likely to use these kinds of methods in their interactions with other people. They will also expect others to treat them in this way. If someone is disrespectful or inappropriate in her response to your children, the difference in the way they are being treated will be a red flag for your children that something is wrong.

When children are young, a more general approach for like or dislike and appropriate or inappropriate touches is a good beginning for teaching your children about sexual abuse. It is also important to focus on teaching them to talk to you when something happens rather than just trying to prevent sexual abuse. As children reach the age for discussions about puberty, more detailed lessons in sexual abuse, harassment, and rape will become part of your sex education for your children.

Indicators of Sexual Abuse

Parents should know the symptoms or indicators of sexual abuse. Having this knowledge will give you an idea of what behaviors you might expect of a sexually abused child. When a child displays multiple symptoms, you should seek counseling for the child because sexual abuse may have occurred. If a child only displays one or two symptoms, other factors outside of abuse may have contributed to the behavior. Typical symptoms you may notice are wetting the bed when it was not a previous problem, an increase in nightmares, fear of being alone with a particular person, knowledge of body parts or sexual positions that are not age appropriate, or depression (see "What is Child Abuse and Neglect?"; Haffner, *From Diapers to Dating*). For older girls, pregnancy may be an indicator of sexual abuse. Genital scars can also be an indicator of sexual abuse but will most likely not be something observable to you. If a doctor remarks on an abnormality in a child's genitals and the child is exhibiting other symptoms, you may want to seek professional help.

Sexual abuse or molestation can happen in all age groups. Some sexual abuse may occur during child sex play (playing doctor). However, children more than three years apart generally don't engage in sex play. We already discussed age-appropriate child curiosity and sex play. While most child sex play is harmless and curious, there are a few indicators of child abuse during this type of play. If there is oral-genital contact, pretend or real intercourse, or finger or other objects being inserted in vaginal or anal openings, the play is not harmless. If the children are giggly and happy during sex play, this is generally harmless play. If they are withdrawn or scared, it is not harmless. Also, sex play and similar behavior should stop after parental discussion with the child. If it doesn't stop, there is a possibility the child has been exposed to inappropriate sexual images or sexual abuse (see Haffner, *From Diapers to Dating*).

Children may also be coerced into sex play. You can ask your children, "Was it fun for everyone? Did you enjoy this playtime? Did anyone ask for the game to stop?" You can talk to your children about respecting bodies and that it isn't respectful if they didn't want to play or other children didn't want to play (it isn't a respectful or appropriate form of play anyway, but respect for other's bodies is a bigger issue when one child didn't want to play or it wasn't fun for everyone). You can encourage your children to suggest another game to play if they become uncomfortable. Make sure your children know they can always call you to come and pick them up if they feel too uncomfortable with a particular game. It's wise for your children to know your phone number and how to dial.

What to Do if You Suspect Sexual Abuse

If you suspect your children have been sexually abused, first remain calm. Your children have taken a big step in coming to you and telling you what happened. They may fear that you will be upset and feel it is their fault. Reassure them that this is *not* their fault and take a moment to praise them for coming to you. If it happens again, they will remember the support they received. Many children try to tell an adult but are confronted with the denial of the trusted adult. My mom confided that as a child she had tried to let her parents know what was happening to her but didn't feel like she had found a listening ear. The abuse continued for a long time because she didn't feel she had anyone else to tell.

Second, be careful to avoid jumping to conclusions about what happened. Children take time (from minutes to months) telling the details about what happened and may have a hard time knowing what to say. Ask questions more than talk, and be careful not to lead your children in the things they are trying to tell you. Remember, this happened to *them*, not you. For example, ask a question such as, "Where did the person touch you that made you uncomfortable?" If you ask, "Did the person touch you in your genitals?" you are leading the children. They may not have been touched in that particular spot but feel the need to say yes because that is what you expect. They love and trust you and want to do the things that will please you or the things they believe you expect of them. If you jump to conclusions, you may miss some important facts or lead your children to unintentionally misinform you.

Next, it is important to use "I" messages when talking with your children. Even if you are not blaming or accusing them, they may feel your disapproval of what happened and interpret it as blame.

If you say, "You worried me when you said he touched you on your buttocks without your pants on," your children may feel some shame about their involvement. If you say, "I was worried when you told me he touched you on your buttocks without your pants on," you are communicating your concern about what happened to the children.

Asking certain questions can also lead children to feel that they are to blame. For example, asking, "Why didn't you tell your friend to stop or run away if you knew you weren't supposed to be doing that?" can make children feel as though they are to blame. You may, in some way, feel your children are to blame for not defending themselves if you have taught them to respect other people's (and their own) bodies. Children are still children and do not have all the reasoning capacity or knowledge to know exactly what to do when placed in a sexual abuse situation. Be sensitive to their tender feelings and realize your children are not to blame.

You may need to contact local authorities or Child Protective Services to make them aware of the incident. If your children need counseling, talk with your bishop or another professional and get your children the help they need as quickly as possible.

Last, treat your children as you have always treated them. If you treat them as though they are breakable or victims, you can compound the problem. Kiss them and hug them as they have always been kissed and hugged. Expect them to follow rules and participate in the family as always. You may have to be sensitive to certain things that may upset them or cause them to remember the abuse, but in general, keep their routine and expectations as they were before knowledge of the abuse.

Sexual Harassment

Sexual harassment includes many types of behaviors and language. It can be lewd staring, inappropriate notes or calls, teasing that includes sexual remarks or jokes, inappropriate names for males or females (doll, hottie, babe), any sexual comments that make a person uncomfortable (it can just be overheard while passing in a hall or in direct conversation), personal questions about sex, unwanted sexual touches, spreading sexual rumors about someone, and other similar behavior. It can also include demeaning women or men in behavior or language. For example, in high school I was the only female in our driving group for drivers training. My teacher called me "little woman" but referred to the males by their names. His comment was not sexual, but it was offensive and demeaning for me. This is considered sexual harassment.

Your children *will* be dealing with sexual harassment in school. Sexual harassment is pervasive in society and is evident in the lewd jokes, stares, and comments made in middle schools, junior high, and high schools. It is common for youth to "tease" one another about the changes in their bodies during puberty. However, this is considered sexual harassment. Teasing is hurtful and uncomfortable, especially during such a confusing time where so many changes are happening. Explain the definition of sexual harassment. Remind your children that they can change the subject or walk away if they are in a group that is treating sexuality or bodies in a demeaning way. They can also say, "I don't think that is funny," when a sexual joke is made. Keep in mind that if *you* listen to jokes that treat sexuality lightly, you are sending a mixed message to your children. If children have been taught that the body is a great gift and have a spiritual reverence and respect for all bodies and spirits, they will desire to avoid these comments and make friends who will treat others with respect and kindness in words and actions.

Rape

Teenagers have many misconceptions about rape. One topic I taught in a marriage and family relations course was relationship violence. I asked the students how many thought most rapes were associated with date rape drugs. About two-thirds of the students raised their hands. They were shocked to learn that date rape drugs are only used in a small percentage of rape cases (see Kilpatrick, Resnick, Ruggiero, Conoscenti, and McCauley, "Drug-Facilitated, Incapacitated, and Forcible Rape"). The media is adept at capturing extreme cases of date rape and creating an altered perception of reality. Teenagers see the media, are sadly misinformed, and tend to believe rape happens with date rape drugs and the perpetrator is someone unknown to the victim. Youth will be seeing rape in the media, hear about it at school, and/or know someone personally who was affected by rape. Make sure your youth understand that date rape usually occurs with someone they knows. That is why it is called date rape or acquaintance rape. It is important to talk with your youth about three different rape topics: avoiding rape, what to do in a situation where someone is attempting to rape them, and what to do if they are raped.

First, teach your youth how to avoid rape. Rape occurs often in situations that involve impaired judgment, such as drinking alcohol or using drugs. Even if your youth is not partaking of alcohol or drugs, there is an increased risk of rape when a youth is in an area or at a party where alcohol or drugs are being used. It is wise to remind them to not accept open drinks at big parties, even from people they know. It is sensible to make sure the seal on a drink is unbroken before consuming it and then to keep the drink in close sight or hand at all times.

Another piece of counsel for dating youth and young adults is to go to a public place when dating someone for the first time. When I was in college, a young man approached me in the library and we began talking. He asked for a date after we had a lengthy conversation. I agreed to the date on the condition that we double date with one of my friends. She was unable to come at the last minute. When I met him I insisted that I drive where we were going and that it be a public place because my friend was unable to come. The young man seemed a little affronted, but we still went out. During the course of conversation throughout dinner he indicated his desire to show me his place. I was beginning to feel uncomfortable with him because some of his questions and comments seemed inappropriate. I told him I would drop him off at our meeting place and call it a night. Because I had driven and we were in a public place, I worried less about what he could do to me. I had power to take control of the date when I started to feel uncomfortable. I could have even left him at the restaurant if I was that concerned!

It's not always necessary to have your youth be the driver, but it is wise to give them a cell phone so they can call if things are beginning to feel uncomfortable. It is also wise to tell them that a date can end at *any* time they desire. They do not have to finish dinner, a movie, or any activity if they feel uncomfortable.

Teach your children to listen and speak up! Because we see in the media two people overcome by passion and having sex or a man coercing, but not quite forcing, a woman into sex, it appears that there doesn't need to be vocal consent to have sex in our society. Teach your youth to be forceful and firm if someone is getting too physical. Push the person away and loudly protest. Being polite or gently telling someone you don't want to go that far may be interpreted differently than expected. Likewise, there is a societal myth that when a girl says no she actually means yes. It is pervasive in media. For example, in *Pride & Prejudice: A Latter-day Comedy* (Faller and Black, 2003), one character proposes to the lead female. She closes the ring case, indicating a gentle no. The male then says, "My mom says that sometimes when a girl says no, she means yes." The female lead had to then clarify herself and say, "Well, I mean no." This case is not sexual but indicative of societal attitude.

Another way to avoid rape is group dating. *For the Strength of Youth* counsels youth to group date during their first years of dating. One reason for this counsel, I believe, is to help youth not only avoid getting too intimate with one person too young but also to gain dating experience in an environment where there is less risk of making mistakes. When I was a youth, I do not believe I would have had the confidence with dating or experience to leave the dating situation I described where I felt uncomfortable. Because I was in college and had experienced multiple and various dating situations, I was able to make a wise decision during a dating experience. Let your youth know that group dating is to protect them from harm and to help them gain experience with the wonderful world of dating.

Next, teach your youth what to do in the event someone is trying to rape them. President David O. McKay stated, "Your virtue is worth more than your life. Please, young folk, preserve your virtue even if you lose your lives" (Kimball, *The Miracle of Forgiveness*, 63). I do not believe that President McKay necessarily intended rape victims fight to the death. I believe he is first referring to our responsibility to prevent scenarios where our virtue is challenged. I believe he is reminding us that we should protect our virtue as the most important thing next to our life. This means that whatever fight you can make in a rape situation, make it. Yell and holler and kick and flail. However, if your life or the life of someone else is at stake, make a spiritual judgment about what to do. Teach your youth to pray for help and guidance if they find themselves in a rape situation. This is sometimes difficult because fear of what is happening, the power of the perpetrator, and the quickness of the event prevents a victim of rape from thinking clearly and rationally in the moment. Also, inexperience and incomplete knowledge can prevent youth from knowing what to do during a rape.

Last, if rape does occur, regardless of the circumstances, make sure your youth knows it is *not* their fault. They may be upset because it occurred during a time where they were breaking a rule or they had been warned by friends about the particular person with whom they were on a date. They may feel it is their fault. Again, regardless of the circumstances, rape is *not* the victim's fault. Let your youth know that there are steps they can and should take if they are raped. Some of these suggestions may be embarrassing and difficult for a rape victim. Tell your youth that it will be hard for them to talk about but that it is necessary to let someone know right away that they have been raped.

To maximize evidence of the rape, counsel your youth to *not* wash the clothes they were wearing. They will also need to see a doctor immediately; it may be best to avoid showering until a doctor can be seen. There may be special doctors or clinics in your area for rape victims. They are sensitive to what your youth may have experienced and have knowledge about any medical procedures that you might need to discuss with your child. Most important, make sure your youth gets counseling from a professional. Talking with a bishop may also help them understand the Atonement and heal spiritually.

Summary

Young children should be taught the sanctity of the body, simple ways to express their likes and dislikes in touching, and what constitutes appropriate and inappropriate touches. You should explain the definitions of sexual abuse, harassment, and rape for your pre-teen child. This should be done after much prayer and consideration. Your child may need a simple or more complex explanation depending on their experiences. If you feel that one issue does not need to be explained, leave it alone until you feel it is time to discuss it. Keep in mind that just because a subject is uncomfortable doesn't mean the Spirit is telling you to avoid discussing it. Sexual abuse is not a comfortable subject. Use the Spirit to know when you should talk with your child and what you need to say. You *will* need to address *each* of these issues with your child. It is up to you, as a parent, to determine the right timing.

24

Sexual Abuse: Questions, Answers, and Ideas

"But whoso shall offend one of these little ones which believe in me, it were better for him that a millstone were hanged about his neck, and that he were drowned in the depth of the sea."

—Matthew 18:6

Question and Answer

Q: What is sexual abuse?

A: Sexual abuse of a child can take many forms. Sexual contact of a child with an adult or other child might be the simplest definition. However, it can include using a child for sexual stimulation, viewing a child naked for sexual pleasure, pressuring a child to participate in sexual activities, exposing a child to nudity, exposing a child to or having a child participate in pornography, or other inappropriate sexual activities. If the sexual abuse is child-to-child, rather than adult-to-child, there is usually an age difference of three years or more. Also, sex play can be considered child abuse if the child is coerced to do something sexual, including viewing or touching genitals with another child. A child can be defined as a person 18 years old and younger.

Note: I use child molestation and child sexual abuse interchangeably. Some argue that there is a technical difference, but they are often used in the same context. Therefore, I did not distinguish between the minor differences in definition.

V: Bodies are so sacred that it is never appropriate to touch someone's genitals or someone to touch your genitals unless it is for cleaning (young children) or medical purposes or unless you are married.

Q: What is sexual harassment?

A: Sexual harassment includes many types of behaviors and language. It can be lewd staring, inappropriate notes or calls, teasing that includes sexual remarks or jokes, inappropriate names for males or females (for example, doll, hottie, babe), any sexual comments that make a person uncomfortable (it can be just overheard while passing in a hall, or in direct conversation), personal questions about sex, unwanted sexual touches, spreading sexual rumors about someone, and other similar behavior.

V: It is inappropriate to make any comments about others, sexual or otherwise, that are directed or intended to make fun of, demean, or belittle body parts or gender identity. We are all children of God in whose image we are created. All bodies are to be treated respectfully in word and action.

Q: What is rape?

A: Rape is sexual intercourse that is forced or unwanted. If sexual intercourse is unwelcome, it is rape, even if you don't say no. Fighting to stop someone from having intercourse is an indication of saying no. If date rape drugs are used and you are unconscious, you can't say no, but it is still rape.

V: It is never appropriate for someone to touch you sexually without your consent. Yell and holler if someone is trying to rape you. Fight as much as you can to draw attention or free yourself from your attacker. However, if someone does happen to rape you, it is not your fault. Get help as soon as you can.

V: It is never appropriate to touch someone sexually without their consent. Sometimes you assume there is consent because kissing or other touching is leading to intercourse and the other touching has seemed consensual with the other person. You should always seek verbal consent before touching someone sexually.

Conclusion

"The temple is a place of holiness. It is the most sacred and holy place on earth and should be treated with the greatest degree of reverence and respect."

—L. Lionel Kendrick

If you have ever studied the pictures on the covers of *For the Strength of Youth*, *Duty to God*, and *Young Women Personal Progress*, you would notice that each displays a picture of the temple. The threefold mission of the Church is "first, to teach the gospel to the world; second, to strengthen the membership of The Church wherever they may be; third, to move forward the work of salvation for the dead" (Benson, "A Sacred Responsibility," para. 14). In each of these pieces of the mission of the Church of Jesus Christ of Latter-day Saints, we find attention to the temple part of the work of accomplishing that element of the mission. First, teaching the gospel to the world is finding people who will then be directed to the house of the Lord for covenants that will bind them to Heavenly Father and further the work toward their own salvation. Second, strengthening the members of the Church includes helping them make and keep covenants that occur in the temple. These covenants guide and protect members, which strengthens them. Third, salvation for the dead occurs in the temple. There is no other building besides the temple that is dedicated to the work of saving the dead.

A temple is a sacred, holy structure where events of eternal significance take place. Our bodies are also sacred, holy structures where events of eternal significance take place. These events can be anything from controlling our carnal appetites to participating in creating new life. I find it interesting that as the Lord describes the body He declares, "Know ye not that your body *is* the temple of the Holy Ghost which is in you?" (1 Corinthians 6:19, italics added). When we use *as* in describing something, we are comparing a feature of one thing that looks like or is like something else. For example, when someone says, "thick as molasses," they are describing something with a property similar to molasses. When we say something *is*, we mean the entity or wholeness of something is not just like but *is* the thing for which we are describing. For example, when we say, "The rose *is* red," we are describing the actual rose. We are not comparing a feature, like saying, "The rose was as red as blood." Thinking of your body *as* a temple gives an incomplete understanding of what the body truly *is*. Our bodies are not just as beautiful as a temple. Our bodies are not just as sacred as a temple. Our bodies don't just have properties similar to a temple; our bodies are temples. My body *is* a temple. Your body *is* a temple. Your child's body *is* a temple; teach them how to use it!

Additional Resource List

"Trust only movement. Life happens at the level of events, not of words. Trust movement."

—Alfred Adler

I have listed some helpful websites for parents and youth, books for children, youth, and parents, and other resources. Please keep in mind that these resources give you, as a parent, a list for finding the information you want to share with your child in the way you feel most comfortable. The intention of this list is not to be all-inclusive but to give parents a resource in a situation where they need to find information quickly or just want to find more information. These resources may change over time, such as website addresses or web pages. If you need to find a particular organization and the web page or address has changed, you can use a search engine to find the most current information (the name of the organization is included next to the website address). Also, parents should always thoroughly check the content of a resource before they read a book to a child, refer a child to a website, or show a video to a child.

Websites for Parents

***Advocates for Youth* (http://www.advocatesforyouth.org)**

My favorite parts of this website include the list for helping your child have a healthy body image ("Ten Tips for Raising Kids with a Healthy Body Image"), the newsletters for parents following sexuality issues for various ages ("There's No Place Like Home … for Sex Education"), and the guide for using media to begin discussions about sexuality issues ("Talking with TV: A Guide to Starting Dialogue with Youth").

***American Social Health Association* (http://www.ashastd.org)**

This website includes information on self-image, healthy relationships, how to talk with a health care provider, and more. They have sections broken down for different age groups. Some information is appropriate for teens, but you should check and decide what parts of the website you will allow your teenage child to view. Some information will be helpful for your engaged young adult. There is also information if your child is asking, "When do you know if you are ready for sex?" (Remember this question may not mean your child is thinking of engaging in sex, but may need information for other reasons.)

***Answer Sex Ed, Honestly* (http://answer.rutgers.edu/)**

This website has a more comprehensive list of resources for parents looking for more books, organizations, or websites. Parents may find this website useful if they are looking for books under a specific category, such as families, gender roles, or anatomy (click on "Resources for Parents," then "Books").

***Child Molestation Research and Prevention Institute* (www.childmolestationprevention.org)**

This website gives some good facts and information on abusers and child molestation. It also includes some peer-reviewed research on child abuse/molestation.

***Kids Health* (http://kidshealth.org/)**

This website has different areas for children, teens, and parents. The parent section has information that may be helpful as you guide your engaged young adult. They can look at the growth and development section for information about current birth control and pregnancy. Under the growth and development icon, there is also information addressing normal sexual and pubertal development.

Planned Parenthood **(http://www.plannedparenthood.org)**

This website has a page entitled "Tools for Parents." It has a lot of information and resources for parents. There is also a different website (www.teenwire.com) that is part of Planned Parenthood written directly for teens.

Rape, Abuse, and Incest National Network **(www.rainn.org)**

This website gives information relating to rape, abuse, and incest. By clicking on the "Get Information" icon, parents have access to information about teaching their teen what rape is, how to avoid rape, what to do if they are raped, and other resources for abuse and incest. You may consider sharing this website with your teen. They may need it or know a friend that needs it.

ReCAPP (Resource Center for Adolescent Pregnancy Prevention) **(http://www.etr.org/recapp/)**

This website is part of the ETR (Education, Training, Research) Associates organization. I especially like the "Learning Activities" icon. You can then choose from a wide number of issues to discuss with your teen. Or you can use it to research answers to questions. This website is great because it is based on research and focused on education. Some of the topics are active listening, friendship, love, contraception, and helping a friend who has been sexually abused. These and many more topics are set up in a "teaching" format, like a lesson plan. These can be modified for parental teaching and would be incredibly useful if there is a topic you want to formally address with your teenager.

Sex Information and Education Council of Canada **(http://www.sieccan.org)**

This website has links for more websites regarding youth sexuality. There is an informational article entitled "Sexual Health Education in the Schools: Questions and Answers." This answers many questions that parents may have about sex education in school. It is a Canadian website, but I believe the information is still helpful and relevant for many American youth in school. This article can be found by clicking on the "Resources" icon.

Sexuality and U **(http://sexualityandu.ca/)**

This website has great information for teens and parents. It includes information on the following (and more): addressing how parents can help teens know about sexual readiness, sexual abuse and coercion, preventing risky sexual activity, sex and the media, homosexuality, and how parents can influence their child's decisions.

Sexuality Information and Education Council of the United States **(http://www.sexedlibrary.org; part of the SIECUS website, http://www.siecus.org)**

This website has lesson plans for teaching sexuality. The SIECUS website is mostly for educators but also has resources for parents. There is a more comprehensive list of books, websites, and video resources for parents. The lesson plans may also be useful for parents to know what is being taught to their child in the school system. You can then supplement where needed.

Talk with Your Kids **(http://www.talkwithyourkids.org/)**

This website is for parents and teens. There is information on relationships as well as sex and sexual health.

Teaching Sexual Health **(http://www.teachingsexualhealth.ca)**

This website is based on a school curriculum in Alberta. It has useful worksheets and information for parents. It also includes information on supplementing school curricula.

Mormons and Gays **(http://www.mormonsandgays.org/)**

This website is approved by The Church of Jesus Christ of Latter-day Saints and is dedicated to dealing kindly with those who struggle with same-sex attraction. It may also be appropriate if you have a child that needs some additional information or support if they are experiencing homosexual feelings.

Websites for Teens

I Wanna Know **(www.iwannaknow.org)**

This website is specifically for teens and is part of the American Sexual Health Association. There are quizzes about sexual myths and facts. There is also information about teen pregnancy and parenthood.

***Kids Health* (http://kidshealth.org/)**

This website addresses a variety of teen issues. It includes some non-sexual information that can be helpful for your teenager, like school and jobs, food and fitness, and a teen's mind (feelings and emotions, feeling sad, mental health, dealing with problems, and so on).

***Planned Parenthood* (http://plannedparenthood.org/info-for-teens/)**

This website includes lots of information and answers to common questions for teens. It is simple, direct, and broad. It covers a lot of information. It is probably one of my favorites for common teen questions.

***Sexuality and U* (http://sexualityandu.ca/)**

This website has great information for teens about knowing when they are ready for sex, what a healthy relationship entails, sexual assault, and what is involved in real love.

***Stayteen.org* (http://www.stayteen.org)**

This website is part of the National Campaign to Prevent Teen Pregnancy but is geared toward teens specifically. The National Campaign to Prevent Teen Pregnancy website is geared more for professionals and parents.

***Talk With Your Kids* (http://www.talkwithyourkids.org/)**

This website is for parents and teens. There is information on relationships, as well as sex and sexual health. The teen section has information for teens on STDs and birth control. Also, there is a feature where teens can sign up to have information texted to them.

***Teen Advisor* (http://www.teensadvisor.com)**

This website is written for teenagers. Parents can still find useful information, but it is a resource to direct your teenager to when they have sexuality questions.

Books for Children

These are listed by age appropriateness for children, beginning with the youngest age. Ideally, books for children should be read by parents before being shared with a child. The parents can then discuss the content of the book, how or what they feel, and what they want their child to learn from it. Also, books of this nature should be stored in a place where younger children, who are not yet ready for the information, do not have access to them. Many of the books listed can be condensed for a younger child or read with more detailed explanations for an older child. The books can be modified in any way by parents for what they feel their child is ready for and can understand.

***Baby on the Way* by William Sears, Martha Sears, and Christie Watts Kelly (ages 3–8)**

This is a wonderful book to prepare children for a sibling. I believe even younger children, age two, can appreciate some of it. The book describes loving a new baby coming into the family along with how the baby grows in the mother's uterus. It's much more simple and appropriate for younger children. A more detailed book about how a baby grows can be found in a variety of other books listed here.

***Did the Sun Shine Before You Were Born?* by Sol and Judith Gordon (ages 3–7)**

This is one of my favorite books about sex for young children. The pictures in the book are not cartoon. They are drawings of real children. There are no inappropriate pictures. Also, the book puts having children in the context of family, including extended family.

***Some Secrets Hurt: A Story of Healing* by Linda Kay Gardner (ages 3+)**

This is one of very few children's books regarding sexual abuse. It is not too explicit for young children and is written in a way that they can understand there are some touches that are inappropriate. This book may or may not be appropriate for your child, depending on their experiences.

***It's Not the Stork: A Book About Girls, Boys, Babies, Bodies, Families, and Friends* by Robie H. Harris (ages 4–8)**

This book addresses sex and pregnancy. I like the last few pages that address what the author calls "okay" touch and "not okay" touch.

***What to Expect When Mommy's Having a Baby* by Heidi Murkoff (ages 4–8)**

This is another great read for younger children, especially if they are expecting a sibling. For younger children, certain pages can be omitted from reading until they are a little older. For example, there is a page on "How did the baby get in there?" It is not explicit in explaining sexual intercourse; rather it's a good introduction to intercourse that a child may need around age five as a precursor to learning about more detailed intercourse between six and eight years old.

Where Did I Come From? **by Peter Mayle (ages 4–8)**

This book has some good text. I like this book because when it describes lovemaking/sex, the pictures are not as explicit as some other books.

Where Do Babies Come From? A Delightful Look at How Life Begins **by Angela Royston (ages 4–8)**

This is a great first read for younger children. If you feel your child is ready, I believe even a 3-year-old could appreciate this book. It might be appropriate if your 3-year-old child is expecting a sibling.

My Mom's Having A Baby **by Dori Hillestad Butler (ages 6–8)**

This book explains sex as directly associated with having a baby and how the baby grows month-by-month. An addition to this book would be a discussion about how sex is not only for making babies. It's also an expression of love between adults.

Where Do Babies Come From? **by Ruth Hummel (ages 6–8)**

This is the first book in a series written from a religious perspective. I like that God is often part of the process during this book. I also like that one section sets up for the next section. This format makes it easy to give a little information at a time and go forward to the next section when your child is ready.

It's so Amazing! A Book about Eggs, Sperm, Birth, Babies, and Families **by Robie Harris (ages 7+)**

The age recommended by the authors and others is seven and older. However, some of the content may be more appropriate for older children.

Where Do Babies Come From? For Boys Ages 7–9 and Parents*; *Where Do Babies Come From? For Girls Ages 7–9 **by Ruth Hummel (ages 7–9)**

These two books are the next set in a series that address sexuality with God as part of the process.

***Changing Bodies, Changing Lives* by Ruth Bell (ages 12+)**

This is a good general book for teens. It goes over not only puberty and sex but also relationships, friendships, eating disorders, drugs, smoking, alcohol, and a variety of other teen issues.

***It's Perfectly Normal: Changing Bodies, Growing Up, Sex, and Sexual Health* by Robie H. Harris (ages 12+)**

This is a good resource for pubertal teens who may need a resource to refer to on their own. You can look over the older age books and decide which book might fit your teen's needs as they experience puberty.

Books for Parents

Everything You Never Wanted Your Kids to Know about Sex (But Were Afraid They'd Ask) by Justin Richardson and Mark A. Schuster

From Diapers to Dating: A Parent's Guide to Raising Sexually Healthy Children by Debra Haffner

How to Talk with Teens About Love, Relationships, and S-E-X by Amy G. Miron and Charles D. Miron

How to Talk with Your Child About Sexuality: A Parent's Guide by Faye Wattleton and Elisabeth Keiffer (Planned Parenthood)

Kids Ask about Sex: Honest Answers for Every Age edited by Melissa R. Cox (Medical Institute for Sexual Health)

Sexuality: Your Sons and Daughters with Intellectual Disabilities by Karin Melberg Schwier and David Hingsburger

Staying Connected to Your Teenager: How to Keep Them Talking to You and How to Hear What They're Really Saying by Michael Riera

Talking to Your Kids about Sex From Toddlers to Preteens: A Go Parents! Guide by Lauri Berkenkamp and Steven Atkins

Talking to Your Kids about Sex: How to Have a Lifetime of Age-Appropriate Conversations with Your Child about Healthy Sexuality by Mark Laaser

Church-Approved Resources

A Parent's Guide by The Church of Jesus Christ of Latter-day Saints

"Dating and Virtue" by David L. Beck and Elaine S. Dalton (*Ensign*, September 2010, 15–20)

"Dating FAQs" (*New Era*, April 2010, 20–32)

"Dating Versus Hanging Out" by Dallin H. Oaks

For the Strength of Youth by The Church of Jesus Christ of Latter-day Saints

Gospel Principles, Chapter 39: "The Law of Chastity," by The Church of Jesus Christ of Latter-day Saints.

"Guardians of Virtue" by Elaine S. Dalton (*Ensign*, May 2011, 121–124)

"Of Souls, Symbols, and Sacraments" by Jeffrey R. Holland

"Personal Purity through Self-Discipline" (*Aaronic Priesthood Manual 2*, Lesson 25, 91)

"President Kimball Speaks Out on Morality" by Spencer W. Kimball

"Questions and Answers: How Much Kissing Is Too Much?" by Lowell L. Bennion

"Sexual Purity Blesses Our Lives" (*Ensign*, July 2010, 10–11)

"Speaking of Kissing" by Bruce Monson (*New Era*, June 2001, 32)

"Talking with Your Children About Moral Purity" by The Church of Jesus Christ of Latter-day Saints

"To Young Men Only" by Boyd K. Packer

"Unsteady Dating" by JeaNette G. Smith (*New Era*, April 2010, 38–42)

"We Believe in Being Chaste" by David A. Bednar (*Ensign*, May 2013, 41–44)

"What Do Kisses Mean?" by John Bytheway

Resources for Pornography and Media

"Are You Media Smart?" (*Friend*, August 2009, 28)

"Talking to Youth about Pornography" by Dan Gray (*Ensign*, July 2007, 48–51)

The Drug of the New Millenium by Mark Kastleman

What's the Big Deal about Pornography? A Guide for the Internet Generation by Jill C. Manning

Approved Latter-Day Saint Sources for Sexual Abuse and Rape

"Healing the Spiritual Wounds of Sexual Abuse" by Ann F. Pritt (*Ensign*, April 2001, 58)

"Healing the Tragic Scars of Abuse" by Richard G. Scott (*Ensign*, May 1992, 31)

"Let God Judge between Me and Thee" by Rex D. Pinegar (*Ensign*, October 1981, 32)

"Save the Children" by Gordon B. Hinckley (*Ensign*, November 1994, 52)

"To Heal the Shattering Consequences of Abuse" by Richard G. Scott (*Ensign*, May 2008, 40)

Bibliography

A Parent's Guide. Salt Lake City: The Church of Jesus Christ of Latter-day Saints, 1985.

Aaronic Priesthood Manual 2. Salt Lake City: The Church of Jesus Christ of Latter-day Saints, 1993.

All Is Safely Gathered In. Salt Lake City: The Church of Jesus Christ of Latter-day Saints, 2007.

Behold Your Little Ones. Salt Lake City: The Church of Jesus Christ of Latter-day Saints, 2008.

Bennion, Lowell L. "Q&A: Questions and Answers: How Much Kissing Is Too Much?" *New Era,* February 1971.

Benson, Ezra Taft. "A Sacred Responsibility." *Ensign,* May 1986.

Berenstain, Stan, and Jan Berenstain. *The Berenstain Bears Learn about Strangers*. New York: Random House, 1985.

Bytheway, John, and Kim Bytheway. *What We Wish We'd Known When We Were Newlyweds*. Salt Lake City: Bookcraft, 2000.

Bytheway, John. "What Do Kisses Mean?" *New Era,* October 2004.

Collins, Chris, Priya Alagiri, and Todd Summers. "Abstinence Only vs. Comprehensive Sex Education: What Are the Arguments? What Is the Evidence?" AIDS Policy Research Center & Center for AIDS Prevention Studies, 2002.

Crain, William. *Theories of Development: Concepts and Applications.* 4th ed. Upper Saddle River: Prentice-Hall, 200.

Dank, Barry M. "Coming Out in the Gay World." *Psychiatry,* no. 34 (1971): 60–77.

Doctrine and Covenants Institute Student Manual. Salt Lake City: The Church of Jesus Christ of Latter-day Saints, 1981.

Eyre, Linda, and Richard Eyre. *How to Talk to Your Child about Sex: It's Best to Start Early, but It's Never Too Late—A Step-by-Step Guide for Every Age.* New York: St. Martin's Press, 1998.

Eyring, Henry B. "Help Them on Their Way Home." *Ensign*, May 2010, 22–25.

Faller, Jason, and Andrew Black. *Pride and Prejudice: A Latter-day Comedy.* Excel Entertainment Group, 2003.

Finkelhor, David. "Current Information on the Scope and Nature of Child Sexual Abuse." *Sexual Abuse of Children*, no. 4 (1994): 31–53.

For the Strength of Youth. Salt Lake City: The Church of Jesus Christ of Latter-day Saints, 2001.

Fulfilling My Duty to God: For Aaronic Priesthood Holders. Salt Lake City: The Church of Jesus Christ of Latter-day Saints, 2010.

Gospel Principles. Salt Lake City: The Church of Jesus Christ of Latter-day Saints, 2009.

Haffner, Debra W. *From Diapers to Dating: A Parent's Guide to Raising Sexually Healthy Children.* New York: Newmarket Press, 2000.

Handbook 2: Administering the Church. Salt Lake City: The Church of Jesus Christ of Latter-day Saints, 2010.

Karofsky, Peter S., Lan Zeng, and Micharl R. Kosorok. "Relationship between Adolescent-Parental Communication and Initiation of First Intercourse by Adolescents." *Journal of Adolescent Health*, no. 28 (2001): 41–45.

Kendall-Tackett, Kennedy A., and Arthur F. Simon. "Perpetrators and Their Acts: Data from 365 Adults Molested as Children." *Child Abuse and Neglect*, 11 (1987): 237–45.

Kilpatrick, Dean G., Heidi S. Resnick, Kenneth J. Ruggiero, Lauren M. Conoscenti, and Jenna McCauley. "Drug-Facilitated, Incapacitated, and Forcible Rape: A National Study." The National Crime Victims Research and Treatment Center, 2007.

Kimball, Spencer W. "President Kimball Speaks Out on Morality." *Ensign*, November 1980.

Kimball, Spencer W. *The Miracle of Forgiveness*. Salt Lake City: Bookcraft, 1969.

"Kiss and Tell: What Teens Say about Love, Trust, and Other Relationship Stuff." The National Campaign to Prevent Teen and Unplanned Pregnancy. Accessed October 14, 2011. http://www.stayteen.org/whats-your-relationship-reality/kiss.survey.aspx.

LaHaye, Tim, and Beverly LaHaye. *The Act of Marriage: The Beauty of Sexual Love*. Grand Rapids: Zondervan, 1998.

Levkoff, Logan. (2010). "She-Bop & He-Bop: The Importance of Masturbation." *Third Base Ain't What It Used to Be* (blog). http://thirdbase.typepad.com/.

"Love One Another: A Discussion on Same Sex Attraction." *Mormons and Gays,* The Church of Jesus Christ of Latter-day Saints. Accessed November 15, 2013. http://www.mormonsandgays.org/.

Oaks, Dallin H. "Dating Versus Hanging Out." *Ensign*, June 2006.

Packer, Boyd K. "Children." *Ensign*, May 2002.

Packer, Boyd K. *To Young Men Only*. Salt Lake City: The Church of Jesus Christ of Latter-day Saints, 1994.

Planned Parenthood. "Curricula & Manuals." Accessed October 25, 2011. http://www.plannedparenthood.org/resources/curricula-manuals-23515.htm.

Popenoe, David, and Barbara D. Whitehead. "Should We Live Together? What Young Adults Need to Know about Cohabitation before Marriage." The National Marriage Project: The Next Generation Series, 2002.

Richardson, Justin, and Mark A. Schuster. *Everything You Never Wanted Your Kids to Know about Sex (But Were Afraid They'd Ask): The Secrets to Surviving Your Child's Sexual Development from Birth to the Teens.* New York: Three Rivers Press, 2003.

"Sex and Sexuality: Understanding the Difference" Resource Center for Adolescent Pregnancy Prevention. Accessed August 31, 2011, http://recapp.etr.org/recapp/index.cfm?fuseaction=pages.LearningActivitiesDetail&pageID=167&PageTypeID=11.

"Talking with Your Children about Moral Purity." *Ensign*, December 1986, 57.

Teachings of Presidents of the Church: Joseph Smith. Salt Lake City: The Church of Jesus Christ of Latter-day Saints, 2007.

"The Science of Love." *Your Amazing Brain*. Accessed October 27, 2011. http://www.youramazingbrain.org.uk/lovesex/sciencelove.htm.

Thompson, Paul. "Former *Desperate Housewives* Star Neal McDonough 'Fired from TV Series for Refusing to Film Sex Scenes.'" *Mail Online*, April 1, 2010.

True to the Faith. Salt Lake City: The Church of Jesus Christ of Latter-day Saints, 2004.

Uchtdorf, Deiter F. "Temple Blessings." *Ensign*, August 2010, 4–5.

Von Harrison, Grant. *Is Kissing Sinful*? Provo: Keepsake Paperbacks, 1994.

Wattleton, Faye, and Elisabeth Keiffer. *How to Talk with Your Child about Sexuality*. Garden City: Doubleday & Company, 1986.

Webster's New World Dictionary. 4th ed. Edited by Michael Agnes. New York: Simon & Schuster.

"What Is Child Abuse and Neglect? Recognizing the Signs and Symptoms." Child Welfare Information Gateway, 2013.

Young Women Personal Progress: Standing as a Witness of God. Salt Lake City: The Church of Jesus Christ of Latter-day Saints, 2009.